THE SCIENCE AND
STRATEGY OF SQUASH

THE SCIENCE AND STRATEGY OF SQUASH

John O. Truby, Jr.

CHARLES SCRIBNER'S SONS/NEW YORK

Library of Congress Cataloging in Publication Data
Truby, John O., Jr.
   The science and strategy of squash.
   Bibliography: p. 255
   Includes index.
      1. Squash racquets (Game) I. Title.
GV1004.T78   796.34'3   75-6818
ISBN 0-684-14260-0 (cloth)
ISBN 684-15063-8 (paper)

1 3 5 7 9 11 13 15 17 19 V/C 20 18 16 14 12 10 8 6 4 2
1 3 5 7 9 11 13 15 17 19 V/P 20 18 16 14 12 10 8 6 4 2

PRINTED IN THE UNITED STATES OF AMERICA

To three great coaches
who taught me the game of squash—

my father, Ed Reade, and Bill Summers.

CONTENTS

PREFACE

The Science and Strategy of Squash was originally conceived as a book that would explain the fundamentals of squash in a manner the beginner could understand more readily than the often complex presentation of other books on the game. This in itself was important, but soon it became apparent that the greatest problem with the present literature on squash was the absence of an adequate teaching manual for the intermediate and advanced player. The purpose of *The Science and Strategy of Squash,* then, is first of all to provide this much needed text for the better player, but also to present the beginner with a simplified form of instruction which will allow him to improve his game at the fastest possible rate.

In putting this book together, I was fortunate to have the assistance of a number of people. Along with Malcolm Cheung, who provided the photographs, and James Henry and Robert S. Lowery, who did the drawings, players Arif Sarfraz and David Bottger and national champions Betty Constable and Nina Moyer were invaluable. (For the sake of continuity, Messrs. Sarfraz and Bottger were used for all instructional pictures.) Claire Townsend and Philip Caton were also most helpful with editing the manuscript. Besides the coaches whose ideas have been noted, I am indebted to William Summers for the many tips he has given me on how squash should be played. Finally, I would like to thank my father as the man who first taught me to play the game, who suggested I write this book, and who provided me with many comments on how to improve it.

FOREWORD

My introduction to squash came at Harvard under "the fine coach of the team, Jack Barnaby." One day early in my career Jack saw me holding a book on squash in one hand and practicing shots somewhat futilely with the other. When he entered the court to investigate my problem, he found that I was studying from a book written on the English squash game, the techniques of which are completely unrelated to the American game. Between Jack's coaching and systematic application and study of the principles of correct play, I have subsequently improved my game to the point where I have won all of the major squash championships.

Mr. Truby's book will enable squash students to learn the right way to play from a book tailor-made to help their game. It is the most complete work on squash written to date. All strokes and strategy are covered.

Perhaps most impressive is the scientific and systematic approach to squash which is introduced here for the first time. Mr. Truby begins by classifying the seven stroke variables which have the greatest effect upon the three stroke characteristics of power, control, and deception. It is particularly helpful for a player intent upon improving his game to have each shot analyzed in these terms.

Every player familiar with squash will find something in this book which improves his game. The approximately two hundred pictures of correct and incorrect aspects of all shots go a long way in clarifying many aspects of the game that otherwise might be unclear. The book should be read in stages and will be especially advantageous when supplemented with instruction from an experienced teacher. Players with several years of squash experience, in particular, will find this makes an excellent contribution to their game.

In squash every player can develop his own game to as high a level as is consistent with his natural abilities and dedication to improve. This systematic book will show devotees enough of the basics so that their own efforts will be channeled in the right direction.

—VICTOR NIEDERHOFFER

THE SCIENCE AND
STRATEGY OF SQUASH

INTRODUCTION

Perhaps no other sport is as uniquely modern as the game of squash. In a world which is rapidly becoming city-oriented, with all the limitations of space and time that this implies, squash is a game played in a modest-sized room, providing its participants with vigorous exercise in the period of half an hour. Even more important, squash can be played by both men and women of any age. And best of all, the game is great fun.

It is not surprising, then, that squash is growing at a phenomenal rate, both inside and outside the United States. According to rough estimates by the United States Squash Racquets Association, the number of people playing squash in the United States has grown from 100,000 in 1963 to almost 500,000 at present. During this time, the number of courts being used increased 100 percent, from 1,500 to over 3,000. This growth has been duplicated and even exceeded in other countries. For example, in Mexico, there existed only four courts in 1967; now there are over 1,500. Among the most welcome sights in squash has been the increasing interest in the game among women. In the past few years, a number of colleges have begun organized programs, and a strongly supported women's intercollegiate team championship has recently been added to the Howe Cup Tournament. Promising an even brighter future for the game are such developments as the building of public squash courts and the invention of an inexpensive, fold-up court.

A SHORT HISTORY OF SQUASH

With the recent upsurge of interest in squash, one might suspect that it is a relatively new game. Actually, squash was invented in 1850 by students at Harrow School in England. These students enjoyed the game of "racquets" but were unable to play often because of the high cost of building a racquets court. Finally, they developed a softer ball than that used in racquets so that play could occur in smaller and more varied surroundings. This new game was given the name "squash," because of the squashy sound the ball made when it struck the walls.

Squash was introduced to the United States in the 1880s, and once again young students made changes. Seeking a faster game, the boys at St. Paul's School in Concord, New Hampshire, replaced the squashy English ball with a harder, livelier ball. Eventually, an American court, narrower than the English court, evolved, and this difference in size became official in 1930 when American court measurements were regularized.

As in the case of so many other sports, squash began feeling its growing pains in the 1950s and did not boom until the 1960s. In such countries as Great Britain, Australia, the United States, and Mexico, the game has become firmly established as one of the most popular participatory sports. Squash is now being transported to other countries as well, and there is a possibility that the game will become internationally standardized.

THE NATURE OF THE GAME

Like most sports, the game of squash derives its essential concepts from combat. The game is composed of two basic elements: firepower (shotmaking) and mobility. These are the primary tools of play every competitor must develop. But these physical aspects of the game are not the whole story. In order to win the squash battle, the player not only must exhibit a high degree of shotmaking effectiveness and mobility but must also be able to display a higher degree of these elements than his opponent. Thus tactics and strategy, the mental means by which a player increases his own shotmaking effectiveness and mobility, while decreasing those of his opponent, are also relevant and important.

These major similarities of squash to all combat, which determine the general structure and organization of this book, are readily apparent. Yet squash is also a unique form of combat as well. In perhaps no other competitive sport is mobility of such primary importance nor as closely interdependent with firepower (shotmaking). This is true for the same two reasons. First, squash is played within four walls so that all shots, to some extent, return toward center court and the retriever. Consequently, a highly mobile player can return many of his opponent's best shots, since the walls keep the ball within hard-running distance.

Second, squash is a game in which both players seek to gain and keep control of the same center-court area. This spot, called the "T" because it is so marked by the lines which separate the back court

The "T"

into two service boxes, is the optimal point in the entire court from which the player can reach any one shot his opponent might hit. Since only one person can stand on this optimal point at one time, both players are constantly fighting to hold this position so that each will be better able to reach his opponent's shot. Thus, in effect, each player in squash uses his shotmaking ability to gain the T and so control play. Seen in this way, squash is a game of mobility in which control of the vital T position is the end and effective shotmaking is the primary means.

Of course, with all of its similarities to combat, squash is still only a game and must always be played with the goal of safety uppermost in mind. Squash is a very safe game when both players realize the dangerous possibilities inherent in swinging a racket at a ball with another person standing nearby and when they control their swings accordingly. Without this control squash is no longer a game of fairness and etiquette, and much of the value of playing is lost.

MOBILITY

In squash, mobility is defined as the ability to move to the proper body position and location in the court to make a shot. There are three determinants of mobility: (1) controlling the T, (2) anticipation, and (3) quickness.

CONTROLLING THE T

Possession of the vital center-court area, or T, is the single most important factor in achieving a high degree of mobility. Because of the high speed of the game, the player who is merely a foot from the

T-area when his opponent hits the ball probably will lose the point if the shot is at all accurate. Furthermore, because the T is the closest spot in the court from which any one shot can be reached, the player who is standing in this area will reach his opponent's shot sooner than if he were not on the T. With more time to execute his return shot, the player increases his chances of hitting accurately as well as his chances of regaining the vital center-court area. Finally, controlling the T is the only determinant of mobility which allows a player to decrease his opponent's mobility while he increases his own. Since only one player can stand on the T at one time, the player who controls it forces his opponent to play from an inferior court position. As a result, the opponent must run farther each time to reach the ball, and so is less able to hit a shot that will move the player off the T.

Of course, a player cannot simply decide to control the T, since his opponent is trying to do the same. How well any individual will control the T depends upon his ability to accomplish (1) immediate and complete movement to the T-area upon making a shot, (2) effective shotmaking, and (3) proper choice of shots.

A player's ability to control the T is greatly decreased if he fails to move *immediately* and *completely* to the T-area after hitting a shot. The person who hesitates before going to the T is often caught out of position or running the wrong way when his opponent makes a shot. Moreover, failure to move all the way to the T can mean the difference between losing and winning a point. But if the player finds that he has not reached the T before his opponent hits the shot, he should stop where he is, for moving the wrong way is always worse than having to run a little extra distance.

In attempting to gain the all-important control of the T, a player must be careful not to place too much value on actually standing on the T. Such an error is especially common with advanced players who are so concerned with being in the T-area that they fail to move close enough to the ball when making their shot (even though they have the time to do so), and they also begin movement back to the T before completing their swing. The player must remember that the T is only an indication of the approximate best area in which to stand while awaiting *most* of the opponent's shots. Even more important, the player must realize that he controls the T not by physically stationing himself on it, nor by being there longer than his opponent, but by getting close enough to the ball in order to make those shots which will force his opponent to extreme positions in the court.

Effective shotmaking and proper choice of shots, which are problems of execution and tactics respectively, are the other two primary factors which determine a player's ability to control the T. These areas of the game will be discussed in more detail in later chapters, but some general statements can be made now. A player cannot gain the T until he has hit a shot which at least travels elsewhere than through or near the center-court area. But more important, if control of the T is to be maintained, every shot the player hits must have a definite purpose; every shot must be precise enough to keep constant pressure on the opponent. Tactically, control of the T is best achieved when the player knows not only all the shots open to him in a given situation, but also the one shot which probably will win him the point. In both the areas of execution and tactics, the interrelationship between mobility and shotmaking is apparent: Effective shotmaking enables the player to gain the T *and* hold it, since the opponent must run farther to return each successive shot; a high degree of mobility allows the player to reach the ball sooner, hit a better shot, and thus drive the opponent off the T.

ANTICIPATION

Anticipation of the shot the opponent will hit is the second means by which a player can achieve effective mobility, because it enables a player to begin moving to the proper hitting position to return the opponent's shot before it actually has been hit. Sometimes anticipation involves merely knowing which shot the opponent must use in order to win the point or take control of the T. However, in most tactical situations, the opponent could employ a variety of shots to accomplish his purpose. In these cases, the player anticipates by closely watching for any clues to the opponent's intended shot.

The opponent's wrist, feet, and racket face are the best clues to the power and direction of the shot he will hit. A person hitting a hard shot usually will bring his racket back high and far behind him, and will set his feet wide apart in a firm stance. On the other hand, a person hitting a soft shot often will take his racket back low, the wrist level with the knee, and will set his feet close together. The general direction of the shot is indicated by the timing of the break of the wrist. The person who snaps his wrist early probably will send the ball across the court, while a person who snaps his wrist late will hit the ball either along or into the side wall adjacent to him. Of course, the opponent's racket face is ultimately the single determinant of where the ball goes and is the only indicator of the ball's flight that cannot be masked by the opponent. As such, the player is wise to focus most of his attention on this part of the opponent's swing. However, the racket face often moves very fast, and thus the player may find it necessary to redirect his attention to the other indicators just mentioned. In any case, the player can gain the little extra time he needs to hit a better shot if he looks for these clues and no others.

Though anticipation is important, many players make the mistake of watching the opponent so closely that they forget to move to the T position. This usually results in their being far from the ball even though they may have correctly determined which shot the opponent was going to use. It is always better for a player who has just hit the ball to move to the T first, and then try to anticipate the opponent's upcoming shot.

QUICKNESS

Quickness of movement throughout the court is the third major factor contributing to effective mobility. The more quickly the player can move to the ideal hitting position, the more time he will have to get set to hit a good shot. Quickness also allows the player the advantage of being able to retrieve shots which otherwise would have been winners for his opponent.

Although some players have more natural quickness than others, everyone can improve his quickness to a certain degree. In an effort to gain such improvement, a player is wise to employ both of the approaches open to him: he can increase his physical *capacity* through conditioning (discussed later in the section on "Mobility Practice") or he may *maximize* his present physical capacity by using the ready position, and by playing in a state of relaxation. A player in the ready position is in a crouch with the knees bent and the body leaning forward, so that his weight is on the balls of his feet. Because of the major importance of the ready position to each of the strokes, this area of the game will be discussed in more detail in the shot-making section.

But the factor with possibly the greatest effect in maximizing a player's quickness is relaxation. When a player moves from a relaxed but ready position, only those muscles which directly contribute to and cause the movement desired are exerted; exertion of unnecessary and even opposing muscles is prevented, and quicker movement results. Moreover, when a player's muscles are exerted from a relaxed but alert state, exertion itself is most explosive, and thus quicker.[2]

This state of relaxation becomes even more crucial *as* the player is moving to return a shot. The greatest players do not run to the ball; they glide with an efficient grace. This relaxed but lightning-quick style of running is preferred (1) because it is the most efficient and thus quickest movement possible when covering a short distance and (2) because it allows the highest concentration and most accurate stroke due to the least degree of jarring of the body. Even more important is the psychological reason for its use. The player who moves in a relaxed fashion thinks much more clearly and quickly than does the intense and excited runner who has little control over the precision of his movements.

STAMINA

The ability of a person to play with effective mobility over an extended period of time is called stamina. Just as control of the T, anticipation, and quickness enable a player to achieve maximum mobility, so do these factors also enable him to have better stamina. The player who most often controls the T minimizes the distance he must run to make each return, and so prolongs the time that he can play without becoming tired. The better the player anticipates, the less hard running he has to do in order to return his opponent's shots. The quicker the player is, the more effective his shots are, and thus the better his position for returning the next shot. The player who controls the T well has the added advantage of causing a decrease in stamina in his opponent who must run from weak positions to retrieve each shot.

Of course, even the most mobile player must expend a great deal of energy during the course of a match, and this can be costly over the long run. The player who tires easily and who is out of condition is at a distinct disadvantage; he becomes caught in a downward spiral of mobility, and thus of shotmaking effectiveness. As the player tires, he loses quickness and some of his ability to move to the T. His shots become worse, he becomes even less able to regain the T, and as a result, becomes even more tired. The final result could be that a player of high shotmaking ability and mobility at the beginning of a long match finds himself unable to hit a good shot or retrieve even a mediocre shot by his opponent by the end of the match. Thus good conditioning is essential if the player is to achieve maximum stamina. The exercise program in the next section is designed to meet the requirements of proper conditioning and is appropriate for players of every ability.

MOBILITY PRACTICE: CONDITIONING

Any program designed to improve a player's physical condition for squash should accomplish two ends. First, it should increase the player's capacity for quickness of movement. To be sure, quickness is basically an innate talent which cannot be altered drastically; but when altered even to a small degree, it can make a major difference in a player's game. A conditioning program directed toward improving the explosiveness of an individual's reactions can effect this change. Second, the program should improve a player's stamina, or his ability to play with a high level of mobility throughout a match. By mobility, we mean here not merely a player's quickness of movement in the court, but also those more specific, but equally important, elements of the player's swing. Often a player who thinks he is in good shape will suddenly find in the course of a difficult match that his swing movements have lost much of their sharpness, even though his degree of quickness remains high. This is because the swing movements do not *have* to be done exactly right each time for the player's shot to be adequate. As a result, a player unintentionally will neglect to perform these movements correctly as he tires. To prevent this decrease in execution during a match, a player must build up a large *reserve* of strength and energy. A conditioning program consisting of endurance exercises can provide the player with this reserve.

To devise a conditioning program which meets both of these requirements is a difficult task, basically because the type of muscle improvement produced by quickness exercises essentially conflicts with that produced by endurance work.[3] The following program solves this problem in two ways. First, it consists of a few exercises which develop both quickness and stamina in a player at the same time. Second, and more important, it contains a conditioning schedule which emphasizes endurance work at the beginning of the season and at the start of each week and then shifts its emphasis to quickness work as the season and each week progress. In this way, the player builds up his reserve of energy early and then maximizes his quickness for his specific match(es).

A note of warning: Many players make the mistake of trying to improve their physical condition by playing many games in a row. This method is both ineffective and unwise. During the average practice session, a player rests often, and thus does not participate in a concentrated enough form of exercise to greatly improve either his quickness or his stamina. Moreover, when a player tires, he begins to practice improper strokes, and these soon become habit. The correct method of achieving the high mobility needed for good squash is to participate in conditioning exercises *after* playing a few games of high-quality squash. In this way, a player improves his mobility *without* harming his stroke.

MOBILITY EXERCISES

1. *Leg-lift Situps.* Lie down flat on your back, legs extended, arms behind your head. Simultaneously, use your stomach muscles to lift the upper body until it is perpendicular to the floor, while bending the knees so that they touch your chest. Extend your legs again, lie back down, and repeat the process. Continue until the required number of situps have been done.

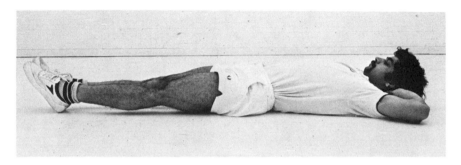

Player lies outstretched.

Player coils, nose touching knees, feet lifted slightly off the ground.

2. *Wind Sprint–Jog Combination*. On a running surface, preferably a circular track, take the proper ready position. Sprint 20 yards, being certain to explode out of the start and to gain top running speed as soon as possible. At the end of 20 yards, slow immediately and jog 20 yards. Then sprint again. Continue this process until the predetermined distance has been covered.

3. *Running Steps*. At top speed, run up approximately 20 to 30 stair steps and then jog down. Do not skip over any steps when going up or down. Repeat the required number of times.

4. *Distance Jogging*. If you are out of shape, begin by jogging only a few hundred yards at first. Work up to one or two miles at your own rate of increase. Do not push yourself too hard or too soon.

CONDITIONING SCHEDULE

The following table is a possible exercise schedule for the course of a normal competitive squash season. It is suggested for young, active players who are serious about their game. However, it is only one possibility and is by no means meant for all players. Older or less serious competitors should keep to the schedule's general guidelines (stamina work at the beginning of each season and of each week, quickness work toward the end of the season and the week), but should work at their own pace. Pushing oneself too hard is not only detrimental to one's game, it is also dangerous to one's health.

CONDITIONING SCHEDULE

WEEK	MONDAY	TUESDAY	WEDNESDAY	THURSDAY	FRIDAY
1	10 Leg lifts Jog 1/2 mile	10 Leg lifts Jog 1/2 mile	10 Leg lifts Jog 1/2 mile	10 Leg lifts Jog 1 mile	15 Leg lifts Jog 1 mile
2	15 Leg lifts Jog 1 mile	15 Leg lifts 25 Step runs	20 Leg lifts Jog 2 miles	20 Leg lifts Jog 1 mile Sprint-jog 220 yds.	20 Leg lifts 20 Step runs Sprint-jog 220 yds.
3	20 Leg lifts Jog 2 miles	20 Leg lifts 25 Step runs	25 Leg lifts Jog 1/2 mile Sprint-jog 420 yds.	25 Leg lifts Jog 1/2 mile Sprint-jog 420 yds.	25 Leg lifts Sprint-jog 420 yds.
4	30 Leg lifts Jog 1 1/2 miles	30 Leg lifts 25 Step runs	35 Leg lifts Jog 1/2 mile Sprint-jog 420 yds.	35 Leg lifts Jog 1/2 mile Sprint-jog 420 yds.	Sprint-jog 220 yds.
5	40 Leg lifts Jog 1 1/2 miles	40 Leg lifts 25 Step runs	40 Leg lifts Jog 1/2 mile Sprint-jog 420 yds.	40 Leg lifts Jog 1/2 mile Sprint-jog 420 yds.	Sprint-jog 220 yds.
6	40 Leg lifts Jog 1 1/2 miles	40 Leg lifts 20 Step runs	40 Leg lifts Jog 1/2 mile Sprint-jog 420 yds.	40 Leg lifts Jog 1/2 mile Sprint-jog 420 yds.	Sprint-jog 220 yds.

Day				
7	40 Leg lifts Jog 1 mile	40 Leg lifts 20 Step runs	40 Leg lifts Jog ½ mile Sprint-jog 420 yds.	40 Leg lifts Jog ½ mile Sprint-jog 420 yds.	Sprint-jog 220 yds.
8	40 Leg lifts Jog 1 mile	40 Leg lifts 20 Step runs	40 Leg lifts Jog ½ mile Sprint-jog 420 yds.	40 Leg lifts Jog ½ mile Sprint-jog 420 yds.	Sprint-jog 220 yds.
9	40 Leg Lifts Jog 1 mile	40 Leg lifts 20 Step runs	40 Leg lifts Jog ½ mile Sprint-jog 420 yds.	40 Leg lifts Jog ½ mile Sprint-jog 420 yds.	Sprint-jog 220 yds.
10	40 Leg lifts Jog 1 mile	40 Leg lifts Jog ½ mile Sprint-jog 420 yds.	40 Leg lifts Jog ½ mile Sprint-jog 420 yds.	40 Leg lifts Jog ½ mile Sprint-jog 420 yds.	Sprint-jog 220 yds.
11	40 Leg lifts Jog 1 mile	40 Leg lifts Jog ½ mile Sprint-jog 420 yds.	40 Leg lifts Jog ½ mile Sprint-jog 420 yds.	40 Leg lifts Jog ½ mile Sprint-jog 420 yds.	Sprint-jog 220 yds.
12	40 Leg lifts Jog 1 mile	40 Leg lifts Jog ½ mile Sprint-jog 420 yds.	40 Leg lifts Jog ½ mile Sprint-jog 420 yds.	40 Leg lifts Jog ½ mile Sprint-jog 420 yds.	Sprint-jog 220 yds.

This schedule is based on the assumption that the player has a match every Saturday, beginning the fourth week. The drill recommended for the Friday of those weeks (220-yard sprint-jog combination) is a light quickness drill and should be used in place of the regularly scheduled exercise any time the player has a match the following day.

SHOTMAKING

STROKE THEORY

Proper stroke technique is a prerequisite to playing top-flight squash. Often a player is superior to his opponent in strategic ability but loses the match because he does not have the shotmaking ability to back up his strategic plans. Even worse is the player who is prevented from improving the level of his game because he failed to learn proper stroke technique when he first began to play. These situations are often due to the player's lack of knowledge of what exactly constitutes proper stroke technique. To provide this knowledge in the clearest and most comprehensive manner possible, there follows a scientific analysis of shotmaking in which only its few most important elements are emphasized.

Every shot in the game of squash displays three basic characteristics to some degree—power, control, and deception:

Power in squash is the degree of force and speed with which the ball is hit.
Control in squash is the degree of accuracy with which the ball is hit.
Deception in squash is the degree to which a player can prevent his opponent from knowing how and where the ball will be hit.

Achieving the ideal stroke depends upon the player's ability to control each of the variables, or body movements, that compose the squash swing in such a way as to ensure that these three characteristics—power, control, and deception—are displayed to the degree desired.

There are seven stroke variables, or movements, which have the greatest effect upon the degree of power, control, and deception exhibited in a particular shot. These movements are divided into two categories, *preswing* and *foreswing*. The preswing movements are those which occur before the forward swing begins, and their purpose is to put the player in the proper position (called the preswing position) to hit a good shot. These consist of (1) facing the side wall, (2) taking the racket back early, and (3) judgment-footwork.

The foreswing movements are those which make up the forward swing of the racket in which the ball is struck. They are (1) kneebend, (2) weight-shift forward, (3) arm movement, and (4) follow-through.

PRESWING

1. *Facing the Side Wall.* For most shots, facing the side wall is the first thing a player does in making a stroke. To achieve maximum quickness, this turning is accomplished by pivoting on the right foot when hitting the ball on the forehand side, and on the left foot when hitting the ball on the backhand side. (All stroke descriptions in this book are based on the assumption that the player is right-handed; left-handed players should reverse these descriptions accordingly.) The ability to hit with great power and control is vastly increased when a player faces the side wall in this way because he is then able to swing the racket across the front of his body, the most natural swing possible. Deception is at its highest because the number of alternative shots the player may hit are increased, and the opponent must wait longer to determine the exact shot the player will hit.

2. *Taking the Racket Back Early.* Taking the racket back occurs simultaneously with the turning of the body to face the side wall. It is of crucial importance that this backswing be complete, the forearm pointing to the back wall, so that no "hitch," or excess backswing movement, occurs as the foreswing begins. The player *then*

runs to meet the ball, with the racket carried behind the body. This position often feels unnatural for beginners who prefer to hold the racket out in front of them at about waist level, but it has an immense effect on power. With his racket back, the player is ready and able to move his whole body into the ball. The player who leaves his racket out in front of him is often caught leaning toward the back wall when hitting a shot because he has had to rush his backswing.

Control and deception are also improved when the player takes his racket back early. By disconnecting the backswing from the foreswing, the player has removed some of the unnecessary motion which can throw off the swing and decrease control. Deception is greater for two reasons. First, when the backswing is not followed immediately by the foreswing, the opponent cannot determine which shot a player

Player pivots
and takes racket
all the way back.

His eyes remain closely fixed
to ball.

will hit by watching the speed and position of his backswing. Second, when the racket is taken back early, the player can wait longer before he begins his foreswing, and the opponent is left in doubt longer as to which shot the player will hit.

Proper preswing position.

Body turned, eyes on ball, racket back.

3. *Judgment-Footwork.* Judgment and footwork are included as one variable because of their interlocking relationship. As the player judges the course of the ball, he moves his feet accordingly so that he will be in the proper position to hit an effective shot.

The stance, the position of the feet during the stroke, is an important part of the judgment-footwork variable because it forms the

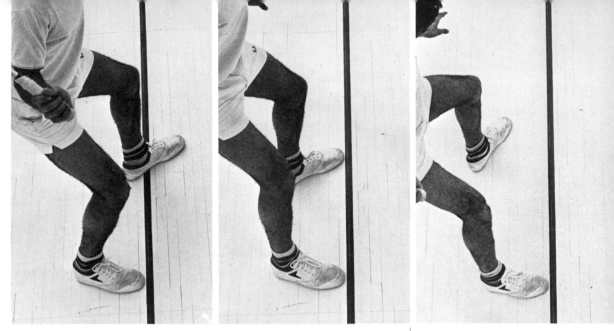

Closed stance. Square stance. Open stance.

base of the stroke. Of the three stances—closed, square, and open—the closed stance is preferred for most strokes since it is the one which provides the greatest potential for power, control, and deception.

Besides the actual swing of the racket, proper judgment-footwork is the only other *necessary* condition to good shotmaking. Even the best swing is useless if the player has misjudged the flight of the ball. The two most costly ways in which this misjudgment can occur are failing to move deep enough to meet the ball, and failing to move with enough quickness. The first error is a case in which improper *judgment,* specifically, moving straight toward the ball regardless of its speed or depth, has become a habit. The second error is a case in which improper *timing,* specifically, moving with only enough speed to just get the racket to the ball, has become a bad habit. In either case, the result is the same: the player is still moving toward the side wall as he hits the ball and therefore is unable to redirect his body weight and motion toward the front wall as he makes his swing. The player must be certain to move back far enough and with enough speed to get set before returning the shot, so that he is able to shift his weight forward and hit the ball in front of his body, at knee level.

Improper judgment: moving directly toward ball without allowing for its speed or depth.

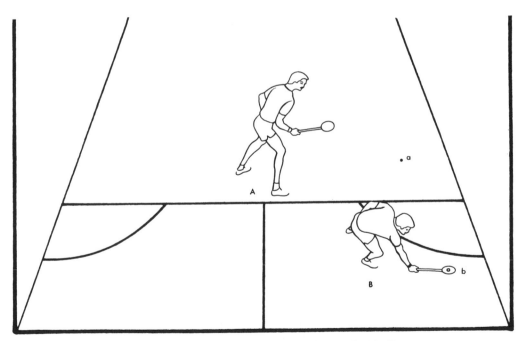

Improper timing: timing one's movement to match speed of ball.

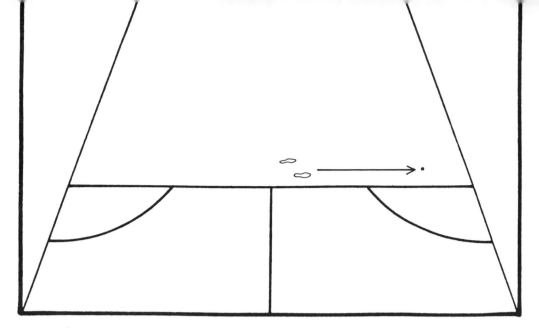

Incorrect: player reaching ball when it is directly opposite from him.

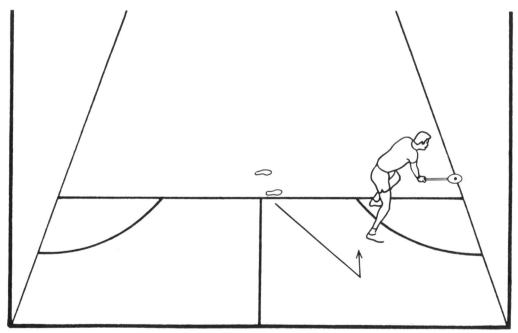

Correct: player moving rapidly to get behind ball before it arrives, then swinging early and leaning forward to hit ball in front of his body.

Unfortunately, there is no way to teach someone how to judge quickly and accurately the flight of the ball; each player must commit himself to the hard task of learning by his own experience. However, there is one bit of advice that can help speed up this difficult learning process. For all intents and purposes, a player judges a moving ball through the use of the bending joints of the body, specifically the knees and the hitting elbow. Usually a new player, and occasionally even an old pro, will move to the ball with his knees relatively straight and his hitting elbow lifted far out from his body. As a result, he usually hits the ball behind his body (due to the backward position of the elbow) as well as too close to himself (due to the straightness of his knees). Proper judgment is most easily accomplished by moving to the ball in a low crouch with the hitting elbow tucked in close to the body. Of course, such movement does not ensure that one's judgment of the ball will be perfect or even adequate, but it makes the prospect more likely.

Concentrating on the ball is another activity of judgment which is difficult to teach but which has an immense effect on a player's shotmaking ability. The difficulty in mastering this area of the game is that a player often will think he is concentrating on the ball but is really not; he is merely watching it. For a player to be concentrating on the ball he must always feel as though he were holding the ball, or "working the ball over," with his eyes. Such intense concentration, of course, ensures that the racket face will strike the ball in just the right way. But it also forces the player to keep his head down and still for a longer period of time during the swing, which, in turn, prevents his shoulders, hips, and knees from opening up, or turning forward to face the front wall too soon. The importance of keeping the head fixed for the proper period of time cannot be overemphasized, but a player who concerns himself with holding his head still only impairs his ability to ready himself for his opponent's return. Instead the player should turn all of his attention to concentrating on the ball, since this not only ensures that he will keep his head down for the necessary distance of the swing but also that he will turn his head toward the front wall when the right time comes.

Player who is executing shot is watching ball but not concentrating on it; notice that his head has begun to turn toward front wall before ball has been struck.

FORESWING

1. *Knee-Bend*. A fast shot cannot be achieved in squash unless the knees are bent. It is the bending of the knees that transmits the weight of the body into and through the ball, thus adding the considerable weight of the body to the strength of the arm and wrist. This knee-bend also provides direction to the ball. In the ground strokes, the highest degree of control is gained when the racket is parallel to the floor. Since the ideal spot to hit the ball on either the forehand or the backhand is approximately the height of the knee, the knees must be bent deeply to allow the wrist to come down to the low plane of the ball, so that the racket can be parallel to the floor when contact is made.

Knee-bend also allows the player to hide the ball from his opponent. When the knees have a pronounced bend during the ground stroke, the body takes a more crouched position, thus making it more difficult for the opponent to see which shot the player is hitting.

Knees bend deeply.

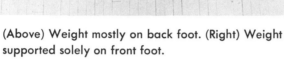
(Above) Weight mostly on back foot. (Right) Weight supported solely on front foot.

2. *Weight-Shift Forward.* Shifting the weight forward, much like bending the knees, is important in all strokes, but is especially so in the ground strokes. The immense effect of shifting the weight from the back leg to the front leg upon the degree of power in the stroke has already been explained. Control, too, is increased, because the player is moving in the direction in which the ball will be hit. A player has greater deception as well, when shifting the body weight forward, because the ball is blocked from the opponent's sight for a longer period of time.

3. *Arm Movement.* The movements of the arm are the primary source of power, control, and deception in squash. The swing is basically a three-part process which begins with the drop of the hitting shoulder, followed by the lead of the elbow, and finally the snap of the wrist. As in the case of judgment-footwork, timing is a primary source of trouble in the arm movements of the foreswing. A costly mistake is failure to begin the swing early enough, in order to con-

tact the ball out in front of the body. This usually results in immediate loss of the point, since the player is then forced to hit the ball late. Of the three individual arm movements comprising the swing, the action of the wrist is of the highest importance. The degree of power, control, and deception of a shot depends largely on the speed, smoothness, and timing with which the wrist whips the racket through the ball.

Elbow is approximately six inches from body, wrist is cocked.

Right shoulder drops, elbow leads, wrist remains cocked.

Wrist begins to snap about four inches from ball.

Wrist snaps at full speed to bring racket head through ball.

Wrist and racket head move far past point of impact.

Racket shaft right next to head.   Racket extended far forward.

Correct

At the higher levels of play, the single stroke factor which distinguishes most clearly the great player from the good one is the difference in position of the axis of the swing relative to the body. With the great player, the swing invariably begins just behind the head and ends far out in front of the body. Consequently, the midpoint of the swing falls approximately six inches *in front* of the player's front knee. With a player of lesser ability, the swing is usually begun far behind the player (especially on the forehand) and then ends just after the player snaps his wrist. The midpoint of this swing falls approximately six inches *behind* the player's front knee. Ironically, this error is usually due to the player's desire to gain more power in his shot, which he improperly attempts to achieve by adding a hitch to his backswing. Instead of hitting with more power, this player only adds a useless flair to his stroke and meanwhile loses power, control, and valuable time.

Incorrect

Racket and wrist far behind body.   Wrist improperly stopping at point of impact.

4. *Follow-Through*. The follow-through, the movement of the racket past its point of impact with the ball, must be correct if the stroke is to achieve the full measure of power, control, and deception desired. For the proper follow-through, the player appears to be reaching for the front wall with his racket. This type of follow-through forces the wrist to move past the point where it whips the racket head through the ball, thus adding more power and direction to the shot.

Racket points to front wall.

Back of hand faces up,
player reaches for front wall.

Even more important, this reaching toward the front wall changes the shape of the swing from circular to linear. Although both types of swing have been used, the linear swing is preferred by far for several reasons. First, in a circular swing, the possibility of error is greater—the player must strike the ball at just the right moment for it to go in the right direction. If a player using a circular swing were to swing just a split-second too early or too late, the ball might travel as much as five feet to the left or right of where it was intended to go. With a linear swing, on the other hand, a small error of judgment might make no difference at all in the path of the ball.

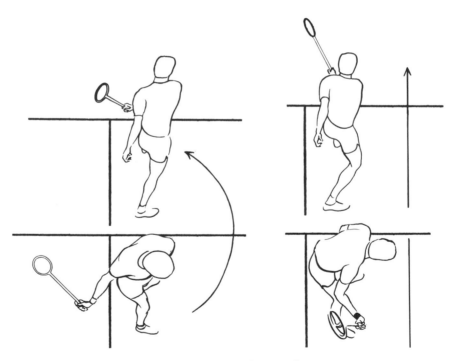

Incorrect: circular swing.   **Correct:** linear swing.

The linear swing is also better for achieving a higher degree of power, because such a swing focuses all the power of the stroke to one point, while the circular swing diffuses it throughout the circular path of the racket head.

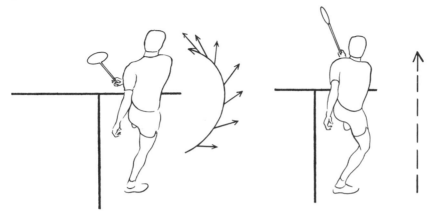

Finally, the circular swing often causes accidents when the racket comes around too far. The linear swing ends with the racket low and pointing toward the front wall. Thus the opponent need not fear being hit with the racket.

In executing the squash stroke, the player must remember above all else that squash is a game won on points scored, and not on beautiful form. Form is taught only because it is usually the best means of winning points in the long run. Players who make stylish shotmaking an end in itself are never the best players. It is not uncommon to see a player approach the ball with the forefinger of his free hand stylishly pointing to the floor and his back foot daintily trailing behind him, who then, upon actually hitting the ball, has his racket face pointing straight to the ceiling. The keynote must always be

The player here has fine form but has failed to accomplish the one crucial task of placing racket face directly behind ball.

pragmatism, and pragmatic play is based on the realization that the racket face is merely a portable wall. Whichever way that portable wall is tilted when the ball rebounds from it determines the direction the ball will travel. If a player is always conscious of the exact tilt of his racket face, and forgets about making certain that all of those graceful gestures have been accomplished before executing his swing, he will always have the best chance of winning both the point and the match.

The same caution is recommended for those players who thrive on the use of power in their games. Often a player will become drunk with the added power that wielding the shafted hitting instrument allows, and therefore will think strictly in terms of swinging the shaft. As a result, the racket face seldom strikes the ball in the right way, thus depriving the player of both an accurate hard shot and an effective short shot. Whether the player enjoys hitting with power or using a more stylish brand of shotmaking, he is wise to follow a basic and very important rule of thumb: the player will always hit the best possible shot for his game if he thinks not of swinging the shaft or of wielding a strong stick but of *placing or, more exactly, throwing the racket face directly onto and through the ball.*

The basic stroke process, which is used for most squash shots, can be summarized in the following simple steps:

1. The simultaneous actions of facing the side wall and taking the racket *all* the way back
2. Movement to the proper preswing position based on proper judgment of the flight of the ball (moving to the ball)
3. Simultaneously:
   a. Bending the knees
   b. Shifting the weight of the body forward
   c. Swinging the arm forward, the elbow leading
4. Follow-through low, wrist moving past the point of impact

It is vitally important that the steps of the process always be done in the above order. A player who attempts to change the correct order of stroke movements will either hit a weak shot or will prevent himself from completing later actions in the stroke, thereby making himself unable to hit the ball at all. The most disastrous example of reordering occurs when the player moves to the ball first and then takes his racket back. In this situation, the player invariably finds that he has less time to take his racket back than he had anticipated. Consequently, depending on the speed of the oncoming ball, the player either hits late or merely pokes at the ball with no power. Preventing this mistake is the first major step to becoming a fine squash player.

INTERRELATIONSHIP OF POWER, CONTROL, AND DECEPTION

The use of scientific analysis has made it possible to determine the seven stroke variables which have the greatest effect upon the three stroke characteristics of power, control, and deception. Such a determination is very helpful in learning to play squash as rapidly and effectively as possible because it enables the player to concentrate on only those seven stroke variables of highest importance.

The accomplishment of these stroke movements constitutes a major part of becoming a good shotmaker, for these movements help the player to gain a higher degree of power, control, and deception in each shot. But simply making these movements is not enough. Not every shot can or should be hit with the highest degree of power, control, and deception. Because of the specific interrelationships of these characteristics, the degree of at least one of the characteristics must suffer when the player attempts to increase another to its fullest. This interrelationship is not necessarily bad; for example, a player does not need, nor should he want, to hit a drop shot with great power. Thus, in order to be a good shotmaker, a player must not merely learn the seven stroke movements but he must also learn to vary them to the proper degree, so that the right combination of power, control, and deception is achieved for each shot.

In studying the basic interrelationships of the stroke characteristics we begin with three hypotheses, determined through careful analysis of the seven stroke variables and our definitions of power, control, and deception, and then follow with a complete explanation of the ramifications of these hypotheses. Once this important interrelationship is understood, the player not only will be able to learn proper shotmaking more rapidly, he also will be able to change his strokes to allow himself more or less power, control, or deception in his shots, when the peculiarities of a particular opponent demand it.

Hypothesis #1 (Power). All other things being equal (natural ability, stroke rhythm, etc.), the highest degree of power in any shot is achieved (1) when all preswing movements have been accomplished early, and (2) when the largest number of contributing foreswing movements occur simultaneously and travel the *greatest* distance in the *shortest* amount of time.

The preswing movements such as facing the side wall, getting the racket back, judging the flight of the ball properly, and assuming the proper stance must be accomplished to furnish the proper base for the shot. Then it is the foreswing movements, such as the bend of the knees, the shifting of the weight, and the snap of the wrist, that provide the real power for the shot. If all of the foreswing movements are used in the stroke, if they occur quickly and simultaneously, and if they move over a great distance, the shot will have maximum power. By the same token, the shot will be less powerful if, for example, the player forgets to bend his knees, or if the bend is slow and very slight.

Hypothesis #2 (Control). All other things being equal, the highest degree of control in any shot is achieved (1) when all preswing movements have been accomplished early, and (2) when the *least* number of contributing body movements travels the *shortest* distance in the *longest* amount of time. Of course, certain provisions must be included: at least one movement, the swing of the racket, must occur, and this movement must not cover too slight a distance nor take too long. These provisions are necessary to ensure that a shot have at least enough power to reach the front wall.

Again, accomplishment of the preswing movements before the arrival of the ball provides the basis for control. Maximum control is then achieved when the forward motion of the arm is the only moving part of the body during the swing, and when its movement covers a relatively short distance over an extended period of time. It should be noted again that such body movements such as the knee-bend improve control, and therefore should be present. The player should not, however, be in the process of making those movements during the swing, but rather should already have accomplished them before the ball arrives.

Hypothesis #3 (Deception). All other things being equal, the highest degree of deception in any shot is achieved (1) when all preswing movements have been accomplished early and (2) when knowledge of the exact way in which all contributing foreswing body movements will act is kept from the opponent for the longest time.

When the player has accomplished all preswing movements, he has a greater choice of shots, and his opponent is necessarily less certain which one he will use. Moreover, the longer the opponent is kept in doubt, the longer he must wait before moving to play the shot, and thus the more difficulty he will have in retrieving it.

One of the best methods of improving deception is to hit all shots off the same stroke—to take the racket back to the same position for every shot. This way, the opponent cannot tell simply by the backswing which shot will be hit. Instead, he must wait until just before the ball is struck to determine whether the shot will be soft or hard, alley, or cross-court.

From these three hypotheses, some interesting interrelationships among power, control, and deception can be drawn which are very useful in learning the game of squash. All three hypotheses show the importance of the player's assuming the proper preswing position early, before the ball arrives. To ensure that he does, the player should always move quickly to the proper hitting position so that he can take the time to hit the most effective shot.

The hypotheses, taken two at a time, are also revealing. Using hypotheses 1 and 2, it is apparent that as the player attempts to improve power, control is lessened. Conversely, if he attempts to increase control, he must hit the ball more slowly. The player can make these changes in many ways, but his attempts will always be of three types: he may vary the *number* of contributing foreswing movements that he uses during the swing; he may vary the *distance* that these movements travel; and he may vary the *speed* at which these movements travel. The degree to which power and control are increased or decreased depends upon the importance of the body movement(s), which are varied. Thus, for example, changing the use of the wrist during the swing has a far greater effect upon power and control than changing the use of the shoulders.

The relationships of deception to power and to control are more complex. The player who attempts to improve deception by waiting longer than usual to begin his foreswing forces himself to swing faster in order to meet the ball at the proper place in front of the body. As a result, power is increased due to a greater explosiveness in the swing. Taken to the extreme, however, this method of hesitating before beginning the swing drastically reduces power, because the player is then physically unable to swing the racket fast enough to meet the ball at the proper spot. Thus, as the player attempts to improve deception, he will also increase his power, *up to a point*. After that, his power will diminish considerably.

Using the same example, we can show that as a player tries to improve deception his control will decrease. By waiting longer to begin his swing, the player forces himself to swing faster, thus hurting control. This loss of control is then accentuated dramatically if the player waits so long to begin his foreswing that the ball goes past the proper impact point in front of the body.

Proper stroke depends first upon the player's doing all seven of the body movements correctly. But it also depends on the player's using just the right combination of power, control, and deception required for a particular shot. A player who understands how to increase a particular shot characteristic can improve his shotmaking merely by knowing which characteristic the shot should display most and then applying his knowledge of stroke theory. For example, a player who wants to improve his offensive half-volley need be aware only that it is primarily a control stroke. From this knowledge, he would then attempt (1) to take the proper preswing position early, and (2) to remove foreswing movements such as a wrist snap, and to shorten and slow his swing. The same systematic method can be applied to strokes that demand more power and more deception as well.

The relationships among the three stroke characteristics can be applied also to strategic situations. For example, a player might find that he is having difficulty in controlling some of his shots or that the style of a particular opponent demands that he play a more controlled game. If he understands stroke theory, he can easily and quickly make the necessary stroke adjustments.

In all of these various interrelationships among power, control, and deception, the degree to which each affects the other differs according to the ability of the player. Thus the expert who has learned to control all of the contributing body movements of the swing extremely well experiences only a slight decrease in accuracy when he hits with great power as compared to when hitting his best touch shot. The beginner, on the other hand, experiences a huge difference in accuracy between a shot that he tries to hit with power and a shot that he tries to hit with control.

For the most part, the reason for this large difference between expert and beginner is practice. Practice of stroke is simply the means by which a player increases his ability to control a greater number of body movements during a longer and faster swing. At the end of the stroke section, a discussion of some efficient practice methods is included so that the player can become an expert squash player as fast as possible.

In the next section this general theory of stroke is applied to the specific strokes used in squash, beginning with the ground strokes and continuing with the volley and half-volley and the serve and return of serve. Each stroke explanation is presented in terms of the seven major stroke variables and is followed by a list of the most common stroke errors. This application of stroke theory is preceded, however, by an analysis of the grip and the ready position, stroke preliminaries which affect the execution of every stroke in the game.

STROKE APPLICATION: PRELIMINARIES

GRIP

The grip is one of the most important components of stroke because it affects every shot. Of the many possible grips, the modified Continental grip (or what amounts to an Eastern backhand grip in tennis) is for several reasons the one which is the most advantageous in squash. First, the Continental grip allows the player to hit the low shots, so common in squash, with greater effectiveness. Second, it is the grip most conducive to hitting the ball with underspin, which is very important because underspin makes the ball die sooner

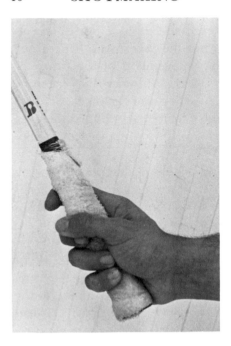

The modified Continental grip.

in the court. Third, it is the grip which enables the wrist to snap with the highest degree of power and control, on both forehand and backhand. Finally, it is the one grip in racket sports by which the player may hit both the forehand and the backhand without changing the position of the fingers. In a game as fast as squash, this is not only an advantage, it is a necessity.

To achieve the proper Continental grip, the player first holds the shaft of the racket with the left hand so that the racket face is perpendicular to the floor. The player then "shakes hands" with the racket, the fingers and the thumb of the right hand clasping the handle at an angle so that arm and racket form almost a straight line. There should be approximately ½ inch of handle showing below the last finger of the hand. The "V" formed by the thumb and index finger rests directly on the ridge to the left of center of the shaft. This position remains the same for shots taken on both the forehand and the backhand.

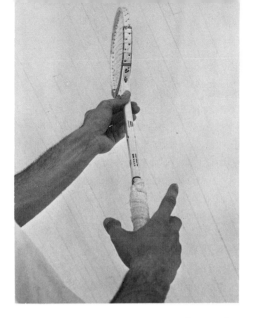

Player "shakes hands" with racket.

"V" of thumb and forefinger is left of center of the shaft.

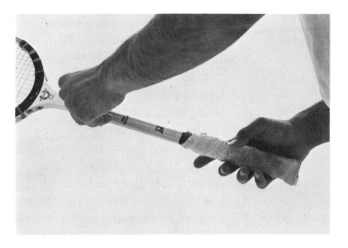

Fingers clasp handle at a sharp angle, forefinger separated from others.

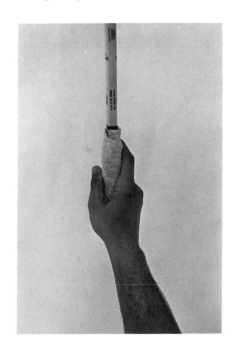

Many players, beginners especially, hold the racket too tight, the result being a loss in both power and control. The racket should always feel as though it were merely an extension of the player's arm rather than an unwieldy club or hammer.

Not all of the fingers of the gripping hand should squeeze the racket with equal pressure. The third and fourth fingers are primarily responsible for holding the racket and, as such, are closer together and apply more pressure than the other two fingers. The middle finger, separated slightly from the last two fingers, holds the racket firmly but not as hard as the third and fourth fingers. The index finger is a full ½ inch from the middle finger. Its sole purpose being to control and direct the racket, it exerts only a delicate pressure so that control will be at its highest.

In general, the grip should be firm but relaxed.

COMMON GRIP ERRORS

1. Employing a tennis forehand grip instead of a squash Continental grip

Incorrect

Correct

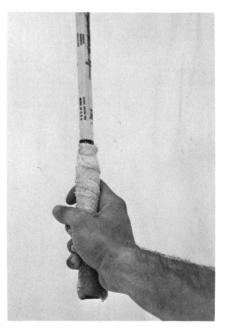 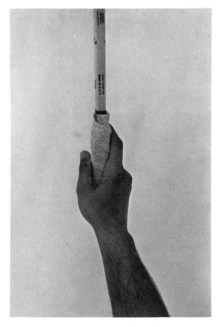

2. Holding the racket as a hammer instead of as an extension of the arm

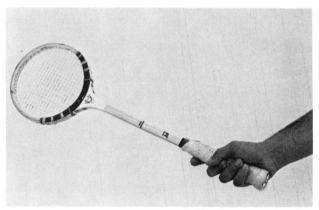

Incorrect   Correct

3. Too much pressure and insufficient spread of the index finger

Incorrect   Correct

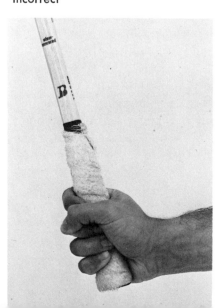

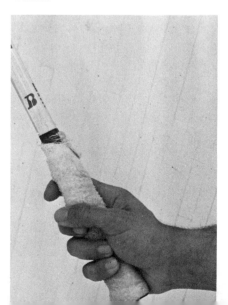

4. Muscles of the hand tensed throughout the entire stroke instead of relaxed until just before the ball is struck

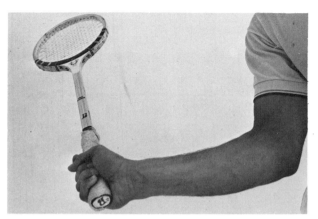 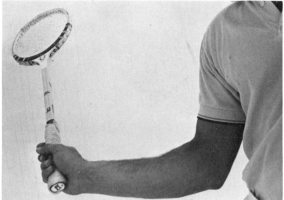

Incorrect   Correct

READY POSITION

Effective shotmaking requires that the player move to the proper preswing position before the ball arrives. But because the player must wait until he is sure what shot his opponent will hit, and because the ball often travels very fast and dies very quickly, the time for such movement is short. Thus (1) the more preswing movements the player can accomplish before the opponent hits his shot, and (2) the quicker he is able to move once the nature of that shot has been determined, the more effective his return will be. The body position that the player assumes while awaiting his opponent's shot and which best fulfills both of these requirements is called the ready position.

To assume the ready position the player stands (usually on the T) with the feet pointing slightly outward. The body is in a crouched position with the shoulders down and the knees bent. Knee-bend is especially important, since it is one of those necessary parts of the swing which can be done early, and since it improves quickness considerably. In this crouched position, the player leans forward, weight on the balls of the feet.

The racket is supported mainly by the grip of the right hand but also by the fingertips of the left hand, positioned on the shaft close to the right hand. To prevent waste of time the racket is held close to the body. The wrist, a primary source of power and control in the swing, is cocked as far back as possible. Moreover it should be cocked *before* the opponent makes his shot so that no time is wasted as the player moves to the proper hitting position. Also to ensure added quickness of movement, both elbows are held close to the body.

From this ready position, the player alertly watches his opponent, who is making a shot. Because an opponent often unknowingly will signal which shot he will use, such careful anticipation can be of great benefit, enabling the player to start forward to reach the preswing position before the ball arrives. However, unless it is done correctly, watching the opponent as he makes his shot can also be dangerous, especially when the opponent is in the back court. The player should be sure to turn his head only slightly, using peripheral vision to view his opponent in the back court.

The ready position.

A final and possibly most important requirement in the ready position is that the player be relaxed while waiting for his opponent's shot. In his efforts to gain maximum quickness, a player will often ensure just the opposite by taking a ready position in which his feet are widely spread and his leg muscles are tensed, as though he were preparing to meet a furious onslaught. The error here is one in which the player has misunderstood the idea behind the ready position; he is using it as a means to protect his immediate small area of the court, rather than as a means to move rapidly to the path along which the ball will travel. When assuming the ready position, the player should feel *not* like a bulldog tenaciously defending its dinner, but like a tiger prepared to spring smoothly and quickly to catch its prey. In this way, the player can explode off the mark and thereby enable himself to defend against shots in the extreme parts of the court, instead of against only those shots which pass nearby. The keynote then is to think of the ready position as a getting-ready-to-move-somewhere-else-position, and to always take a ready position in which the feet are under the body and the leg muscles are relaxed.

COMMON READY POSITION ERRORS

1. Knees stiff and racket down

Incorrect

Correct

2. Body tense instead of relaxed but alert

Incorrect

Correct

3. Leaning or bouncing on the T while waiting for the opponent's shot

Incorrect

Correct

FOREHAND

The forehand is the favorite stroke of most novice players because it allows them to hit with great power. Tactically, the use of a hard shot is effective, especially on deep shots in which speed is very helpful in passing an opponent well positioned on the T. Unfortunately, hitting with a high degree of power means a relative decrease in control, and this often leads to drastic results, especially for beginning and intermediate players. A slight lapse in control on a long deep shot, for example, can cause the ball to hit the side wall during its flight so that it bounces to the middle of the court for an easy putaway by the opponent. The average player should seldom attempt to substitute a high degree of power for control, even in a stroke as potentially powerful as the forehand. Instead, he should begin by hitting a forehand in which power is moderate and control is great, best achieved simply by reducing the speed of the foreswing movements. As he becomes more experienced and better able to control the many stroke variables that go into making a powerful shot, the player can progressively increase the power of his forehand drives while his control remains at the same high level. A particular opponent may necessitate the use of more power and a player must be ready and willing to employ such an attack. But uncontrolled power is seldom effective.

MOVEMENTS TO FOREHAND PRESWING POSITION

Ready Position

1. *Face Side Wall.* The player in the ready position, upon determining that the shot will be taken on the forehand side, pivots on his right foot, thus turning the body so that it faces the side wall.

2. *Get Racket Back Early.* As the player turns to face the side wall, he simultaneously brings the racket back so that the forearm is pointing to the back wall. The racket is perpendicular to the floor, and the racket head is just above the player's head. For most shots, the elbow is approximately 6 inches from the body and the wrist is cocked as far back as possible.

3. *Judgment–Footwork.* The judgment and footwork process already had begun with the player's decision to take the shot on the forehand side. Having turned sideways and taken his racket back, the player continues this process of judgment and footwork by determining the ideal spot in the court where the ball may be hit most effectively and then by moving there as quickly as possible. The ideal spot for hitting a controlled forehand shot is directly opposite the front knee with the ball coming down off its rise after it has bounced on the floor once. When the player has moved to what he believes to be the ideal spot to hit the shot, he sets his feet in a closed stance with his left foot pointing at about a 45° angle to the front wall. Throughout this very short period of time in which the player turns sideways, takes the racket back, and moves to the ideal hitting position, his eyes are concentrated on the oncoming ball. Keeping his head perfectly still, he watches the ball in this manner until the strings of the racket have contacted the ball.

FORESWING

4. *Knee-Bend.* Bend of the knees is very important throughout the preswing period, but it is especially so during the actual foreswing. The body is in a crouch in the ready position and remains this way as the player moves in a low glide to meet the ball. When the player begins the swing, he bends his knees much deeper in order that the racket head remain higher than the wrist when it contacts the ball.

5. *Weight-Shift Forward.* As the player assumes the preswing position, he places his weight mainly on his right foot. As he begins his foreswing, however, he takes a small step forward with his left foot and shifts his weight forward. Weight-shift is transmitted through the knee-bend and this can occur only when the stepping (left) foot is pointing outward (at about a 45° angle). Thus, the player must be certain that he does not commit the common error of stepping with his foot parallel to the back wall, since this prevents both knee-bend and weight-shift.

6. *Arm Movement.* As the ball nears the desired spot just opposite the front knee, the player begins the foreswing, adding *no extra backswing, or hitch, to the stroke.* He simply brings the arm straight forward, dropping the right shoulder lower than the left. The elbow drives forward toward the ball, leading the wrist which continues to be

cocked as far back as possible. When the wrist is just a few inches from the front knee, it snaps quickly and the ball is struck. The open face of the racket head, the lead of the elbow, and the slightly downward plane at which the racket travels in the foreswing all combine to put underspin on the ball. This underspin is vitally important to the shot because it makes the ball jump to the floor quickly, thus increasing the difficulty the opponent has in hitting a return.

It should be noted that the relative position of the elbow to the wrist is a primary difference between the tennis and the squash forehand. In tennis, the elbow follows the wrist, while in squash, the elbow leads the stroke and the wrist follows.

7. *Follow-Through.* In ending the stroke the player "hits through the ball"—that is, he continues the wrist past the point of impact and on toward the front wall. The player should feel in the follow-through as if he were "reaching for the front wall" or "throwing the racket at the front wall." It is also imperative in a good follow-through that the knees remain bent and the racket be low. This enables the player to move back to the ready position on the T quickly and thus be prepared for his opponent's possible return.

COMMON FOREHAND ERRORS

1. Moving to the ball before taking the racket back

Incorrect

Correct

2. Failure to take the racket all the way back at the beginning

Incorrect

Correct

3. Trying to achieve power in the shot in the wrong way—adding a hitch to the foreswing

Incorrect

Correct

4. Failure to move the hips and feet close enough to the ball, thus forcing the racket hand to swing forward too far from the body (the problem is especially common in the advanced player whose ingrained fear of moving too far from the T has made him habitually stop short of the proper hitting position)

Incorrect

Correct

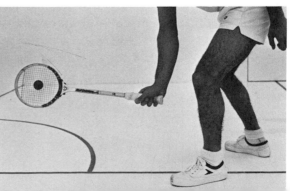

BACKHAND

The backhand in squash is potentially a more powerful stroke than the forehand. In the backhand, the body uncoils rapidly, bringing into the stroke more body movements, and thus more power. Moreover, in the backhand, the front arm does the hitting instead of the rear arm, as in the forehand. Consequently, the player hits the ball farther out in front of his body, resulting in a greater shift of his weight, and thus in a more powerful shot.

But for many of these same reasons, the backhand is the more difficult stroke for a beginner or intermediate player to do correctly. From stroke theory, we know that while a larger number of body movements allow a player potentially more power, they also make control harder to achieve, since the player must execute more movements properly. Hitting the ball with the front arm instead of the rear arm increases power but increases the chance of error as well. On the forehand, if the ball passes the ideal hitting spot, an effective shot is still possible. If this happens on the backhand, however, the player must quickly lean back just to return the ball, much less hit it with power or accuracy. Furthermore, a player performs fewer daily actions with the back of the hand and arm. This results in the bad habit, which most beginners exhibit, of trying to push the ball, rather than stroke it. Improvement is greatly hindered if the backhand ground strokes are habitually done this way, so the player is wise to learn the proper backhand stroke as early as possible.

MOVEMENTS TO BACKHAND PRESWING POSITION

Ready Position

1. *Face Side Wall.* The player pivots on his left foot upon deciding that he will hit the ball with the backhand stroke. Failure to turn the body so that it faces the side wall is a primary reason behind a player's pushing rather than stroking the ball.

2. *Get Racket Back Early.* With the turning of the body, the player brings the racket back so that the forearm is parallel to the floor and points to the back wall. The right shoulder is lower than the left, the elbow is in close to the body, while the wrist is cocked as far back and to the left as possible. While the player is moving to meet the ball, he holds the racket perpendicular to the floor with the racket head just above ear level. As the ball approaches, he moves the wrist higher, just level with the left shoulder, so that the racket is in a diagonal position across the back of the neck. This serves to twist the body around so that it can unwind rapidly for a powerful shot. Again, the player must be certain not to add any hitch to the foreswing motion; in this particular case, failure to separate the upward movement of the wrist from the forward swing of the racket always results in uncontrolled and undisguised power.

3. *Judgment-Footwork.* Facing the side wall with his racket back, the player judges quickly the speed and trajectory of the ball

and then moves immediately to position himself behind it. However, he does not allow the ball to come right at him; the use of a pushing stroke on the backhand instead of the proper stroke is due mainly to improper judgment whereby the player lets the ball come too close to his body. The ball must be kept a racket length away from the right knee if the shot is to be accurate. More-

over, it should be struck approximately 6 inches ahead of the right knee to enable the player to lean adequately into the ball for greater power. As the ball nears this ideal spot, the player sets his feet in the closed stance. Throughout all movement to the preswing position, he keeps close watch on the ball and does so until it has been hit.

FORESWING

4. *Knee-Bend*. In the backhand, as in the forehand, the knees are bent and the body is in a crouched position throughout the stroke. For the actual foreswing, however, the player bends his knees much deeper to allow the wrist to drop down to knee level, so that the shaft of the racket will be parallel to the floor when it strikes the ball.

5. *Weight-Shift Forward*. While the player is moving to the preswing

position, he supports his weight on the left foot. He then shifts his weight from the left foot to the right foot (weight transmitted by the bend of the knees), as he swings and steps forward with his right foot. Again, the stepping foot points outward for pronounced weight shift.

6. *Arm Movement*. To begin the forward swing of the racket, the player draws his elbow forward. Initially, the elbow is bent, but

it rapidly extends so that *arm and racket form a straight line when the ball is struck*. The wrist remains cocked until just after it has passed the front knee, at which point, it snaps quickly and whips the racket head into and through the ball. The player must be careful not to snap his wrist too soon or much of the power of the swing will be lost. Again, underspin is caused by the open face of the racket head and the slightly downward angle of the swing.

7. *Follow-Through*. As the racket strikes the ball, the wrist continues past the point of impact on toward the front wall. The player should again feel as if he were throwing his racket at the front wall, the back of the hand pointing straight up. Contrary to the forehand in which both shoulders face the front wall on the follow-through, in the backhand the shoulders stay closed, facing the side wall. The body remains in its crouched position with shoulders down and knees bent to ensure that the racket ends low and that the player can move back quickly to the ready position on the T.

COMMON BACKHAND ERRORS

1. Beginning the foreswing too late so that the ball is struck behind the body

Correct

Incorrect

2. Allowing the elbow to lead the stroke instead of holding it close to the body

Incorrect   Correct

3. Failure to watch the ball until it has been struck, caused by a desire to see how effective one's own shot has been

Correct

Incorrect

4. Failure to step into the ball with the front foot pointing outward at a 45° angle

Incorrect

Correct

5. Allowing the front knee to straighten so that the racket ends high

Incorrect

Correct

6. Failure to move the feet close enough to the ball to make the shot

Incorrect   Correct

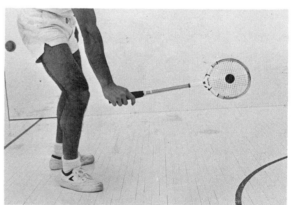

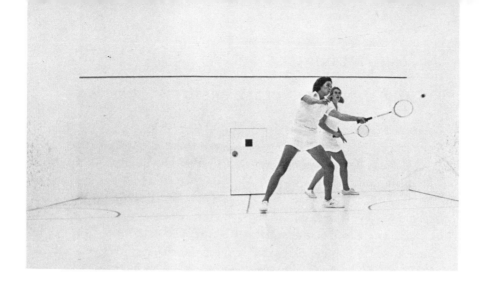

VOLLEY

One of the best means by which a player can win in squash is to force his opponent to run hard for all shots so that he makes less effective returns and many mistakes. Proper volleying does just that, since it drastically shortens the time the opponent has to react and forces him to move to the ball before he has reached the all-important T position. Conversely, the volleyer can keep almost constant control of the T and thus react to his opponent's return more effectively.

But despite the advantages of the volley, it is one of the least-used shots in squash. Because of the great speed at which the ball travels, many players find that they do not have enough time to set properly in order to hit with the high degree of control and power they feel this shot demands. The solution to this problem is two-part. First, since the ball travels very fast, the player must assume the correct ready position so that he achieves maximum quickness. Second, the player must realize that he need not hit the volley with much power or with pinpoint accuracy. Indeed, attempts to do so only lead to errors. Instead, the player should concentrate merely on attacking the ball, hitting far out in front of his body, and aiming at least a foot above the tin at all times. To be sure, the player will not often make an outright winner when volleying in this way. But as the fine coach of the Harvard University team, Jack Barnaby, has said, "An individual volley doesn't look very impressive, but a lot of them have a cumulative effect that can be devastating as the match wears on and the fast pace begins to take effect." [4]

MOVEMENTS TO VOLLEY PRESWING POSITION

Ready Position

1. *Do Not Face Side Wall or Take Racket Back.* The player cannot and must not turn sideways or take his racket back before making the volley; the ball moves too fast. The effect of the volley comes from the immediate and total attack of the forward movement of the body onto the ball. Any attempt to turn sideways and take the racket back only hinders the quickness and thrust of this attack. Some turning of the body is accomplished, however, when the player steps toward the ball just before he begins the forward swing of the racket.

2. *Judgment-Footwork.* The success of a player's volleying game,

Forehand

Backhand

even more than the success of his ground strokes, depends upon his ability both to judge the flight of the ball and to move to the proper place in the court before the ball arrives. The player's sole aim in the judgment-footwork part of the volley is to position himself *behind* the flight of the ball. To do this, he must move very fast.

Ideally, the player should hit the ball farther out in front of the body on the volley than on the ground strokes, since the volley is a more aggressive shot. As usual, the player must watch the ball all the way into the racket strings if the shot is to be effective.

FORESWING

3. *Knee-Bend and Weight-Shift Forward.* The player should keep his knees bent low enough during the swing so that the racket head is always higher than the wrist when the ball is volleyed. Otherwise, the racket head may have to drop to make contact with the ball, resulting in a loss of control, if the opponent's shot is especially low.

Moving the body forward and into the ball is the most important but also the most difficult part of the volley. The basic purpose of using the volley is to rob the opponent of much of the time he needs to retrieve the ball. But often a player defeats this purpose by falling backward when he volleys, in an attempt to give himself more time to con-

Forehand

Backhand

trol the fast-approaching ball. Instead, he should always be leaning forward, attacking the ball, as he swings. It should be noted, however, that the player should *not* shift weight *during* the stroke but rather should already be moving into the ball as the foreswing begins.

4. *Arm Movement.* Arm movement for the volley is all one motion but it is by no means a rapid motion. The player begins the swing early so that he may hit the ball far out in front of the body. With the approach of the ball, the player steps toward it, using the left foot on the forehand and the right foot on the backhand. Simultaneously, he extends the arm and racket upward, forward, and sideways at about a 45-degree angle so that the racket is almost pointing to the ball. At the last instant, he quickly snaps the wrist, bringing the open-faced racket forward in a slightly downward path for underspin.

5. *Follow-Through.* After the ball has been struck, the wrist moves past the point of impact with the ball toward the front wall until the hitting arm is fully extended. The player again should feel as though he were throwing the racket at the front wall. The knees are bent and the racket is low so that the player can move immediately to the ready position on the T.

HALF-VOLLEY

The half-volley—a shot in which the ball is hit just after it has bounced on the floor—can be either a defensive or an offensive shot. Defensively, it is a shot a player uses to avoid immediate loss of the point when he has been caught off-guard. Most players hit the half-volley only as a defensive shot.

Yet, like the volley, the half-volley can be an excellent offensive weapon. The offensive half-volley is used when the ball bounces in the midcourt area in front of the T. It is effective because, like the volley, it steals the time the opponent needs to move to the ball, and causes him to start that movement before he has reached the T.

Very few players use the half-volley offensively because they feel they have too little time to hit the shot with the control it demands. Although there is very little time, the half-volley *can* be executed effectively if the determinants of control are carefully adhered to. According to stroke theory, control is best achieved when no unnecessary motion occurs and when as many different movements as possible are removed from the swing. Consequently, *there is no back-swing* or break in the wrist in the half-volley stroke. The player must also realize that pinpoint accuracy is not necessary to the shot. The half-volley is a good weapon *not* because it hits just above the tin, but because it catches the opponent in the back court. The shot may be aimed as much as a foot and a half above the tin and still be a deadly weapon. To aim lower is to take a high and usually unnecessary risk.

MOVEMENTS TO HALF-VOLLEY PRESWING POSITION

Ready Position

1. *Do Not Turn Sideways or Take Racket Back*. As in the case of the volley, any attempt to face the side wall when making the half-volley is both impossible and undesirable. However, when time permits, the player should again step into the ball with his left foot on the forehand and his right foot on the backhand. This step allows the player to attack the ball and to turn the body partly sideways without wasting time.

2. *Judgment-Footwork*. Because, in the half-volley, the ball is hit just after it bounces on the floor, the possibility for error is great. Thus proper judgment is very important. Again, the player's goal is to position himself behind the flight of the ball. Perhaps most important, the player must watch the ball closely or else he will probably make an error.

Forehand

Backhand

FORESWING

3. *Knee-Bend and Weight-Shift Forward.* For maximum control, the player should bend his knees deeply to allow the wrist to be lower than the racket head when the ball is struck. But if possible, the knee-bend should occur before the ball arrives, because any excess motion during the swing decreases control.

   Similarly, the body should already be leaning forward and moving into the ball as the swing begins. Again, the key to this shot lies in attacking the ball, leaning forward, and hitting the ball far in front of the body.

4. *Arm Movement.* Since the offensive half-volley is almost totally a control stroke, all excess body movement and unnecessary motion must be removed. Thus the player should make no backswing, or hitch, at the last instant before he begins his foreswing. He should swing by merely extending his arm diagonally forward and placing the racket face on the ball. Even more important, the player must keep his wrist locked firmly, for wrist-snap here is dangerous excess motion.

5. *Follow-Through.* While the player hits through the ball in the usual manner, he uses a follow-through for the half-volley which is much shorter than for those of other strokes. Again, the player must stay low so that he can move back to the T position rapidly.

Forehand —————————————————————————————

Backhand —————————————————————————————

COMMON VOLLEY AND HALF-VOLLEY ERRORS

1. Using too big and too hard a swing

Correct

Incorrect

2. Attempting too exact a shot

3. Failure to step forward and hit the ball out in front of the body

Incorrect

Correct

SERVE

The serve is the shot which begins the point, and it also can be the shot which ends the point. Even if it is not an outright winner, a well-placed serve can put the receiver in a difficult position at the start so that the server can control play and eventually win the point.

Unfortunately, many players fail to realize the potential of the serve in winning points. They take little care with their serves, content to use the shot merely to put the ball into play. As a result, it is often the receiver who wins the point outright or who gains the center-court position.

The server's failure to take care with his shot is certainly not due to lack of time, since he is the one who puts the ball into play. The fact that the server has time is one reason that the serve can be such an effective weapon; the server can easily move to the preswing position and make those adjustments which will enable him to hit with more control or more power. Of the three basic types of serve—"lob," "hard," and "slice"—the lob serve is the one which must be hit with the most control to be effective, while the hard serve is obviously the one which must be hit with the most power.

Variation in the serve, as in every tactical situation, is vital to success. Against most opponents in most courts, the player should use the lob serve predominantly, reserving the hard and slice serves for surprise. But if the circumstances—a particular opponent, court, or the player's own ability to hit one serve better than the others—warrant a change in this order, the player is wise to adjust accordingly.

LOB SERVE

The lob serve is a slow, highly arched shot, which ideally hits far up on the front wall, strikes the side wall in the receiver's court a little above head level, and bounces on the floor close to the back wall. The lob is the safest of the three serves; even when the server's aim is a little off, the lob can still be a good serve.

But perhaps most important, the lob best accomplishes the server's purpose of immediately forcing the opponent far out of position so that the server can take the T. The slow speed at which the ball travels and the depth of the court at which the ball must be received give the server ample opportunity to take the T and provide him with a better chance of eventually winning the point.

LOB SERVE PRESWING POSITION

1. *Stance.* From the right service box, the player assumes an open stance (stance is closed when the player serves from the left service box) with one foot, usually the back, placed within the box. The front foot points toward the front wall while the body faces approximately toward the corner formed by the right side wall and the front wall.
2. *Racket Is Back.* The player takes no backswing during the actual serve, since this would reduce control. Instead the racket is held at about waist level and points toward the corner of the right side wall and the back wall. The wrist is cocked and is lower than the racket head, while the elbow is kept close to the body for better control. The ball is held by the fingertips of the left hand, approximately level with the waist.
3. *Judgment.* To be effective, a lob serve must:

   1. Have a high arc so that it falls almost vertically into the opposite court
   2. Strike the side wall of the opposite court approximately level with the receiver's head and a few feet from the back wall
   3. Hit the floor as close to the back wall as possible without actually hitting the back wall first

Each of these requirements demands that the ball strike close to a certain spot on the front wall. Ideally this spot should be close to the top of the front wall and just to the left of center when the player serves from the right and just to the right of center when the player serves from the left. The player watches this

spot after he has assumed the preswing position and has seen that his opponent is ready. Just before he begins the foreswing, he switches his attention to the ball and, as always, watches it closely.

FORESWING

4. *Arm Movement.* As the player swings the racket forward and upward, he drops the ball. He keeps his wrist firmly locked so that wrist-snap, which could cause a decrease in control, does not occur. The racket should contact the ball at about knee level and should come up on the ball to give it topspin. Topspin is used in this specific stroke because it makes the ball travel in a higher arc after it strikes the front wall. Throughout the foreswing, the player stays low to gain better control and to allow his weight to shift forward.

5. *Follow-Through.* Again the player hits through the ball, the racket ending high above the left shoulder, to ensure proper control and topspin. In continuous motion with the follow-through, the player moves immediately to the T; he does not stop to see how well he has executed the serve.

HARD SERVE

The hard serve is an overhead shot that is hit with great power. There are basically three types of hard serves: (1) hard serve at the opponent, (2) hard serve at the opponent's back corner, and (3) hard serve to the T. The stroke for each of these hard serves is the same except that each is aimed at a different spot on the front wall.

Because it is such a fast shot, the hard serve can be very effective at winning a point outright, especially if the receiver is caught by surprise. Yet most players use the hard serve only as an occasional variation from the usual lob. This is so partly because the hard serve can be put away easily if it is not hit quite correctly. Also, the hard serve usually throws the server off balance; thus, against an experienced opponent who can volley, the server often will have lost the point before he has recovered from his swing. Finally, since much of the effectiveness of the hard serve is due to the element of surprise involved, it can become detrimental to the player who uses it too often. As a result most players employ the hard serve only sparingly, but increase its use when the opponent becomes tired, or when a big point is needed.

The following are three types of hard serve:

1. *To Opponent.* This hard serve should be aimed at a spot on the front wall just right of center when the player serves from the right side, and just left of center when the player serves from the left side. In executing the serve, the player must aim high enough on the front wall for the ball to travel all the way to the back wall before striking the floor. However, so that the shot achieves maximum speed, the player should also aim as close to the front-wall service line as his size and strength allow. The player with less strength must aim higher, of course.

If the serve is hit properly so that it moves very fast and hits the back wall close to the floor (or, of course, if it strikes the opponent), it can easily win the point outright. On the other hand, the server risks losing the point outright if the ball bounces on the floor first, since the receiver then controls the vital center-court area and can hit a sure winner.

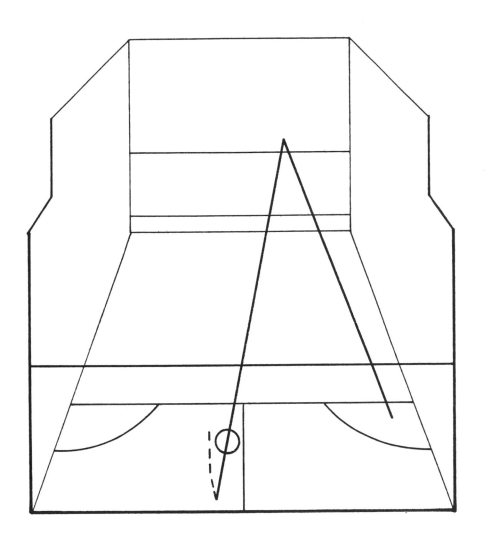

2. *To the Opponent's Back Corner.* This serve should hit just left of center of the front wall when the server is on the right side and just right of center when the server is on the left side. The ball should strike the back wall close to the floor and the side wall. Again, just how high on the front wall the ball is hit depends upon the size and strength of the server.

The hard serve to the opponent's back corner can be devastating if it is hit correctly and is not volleyed. However, if the ball strikes the floor or the side wall before the back wall, or if the opponent is wise enough to volley the shot, this hard serve can be easy prey for the opponent.

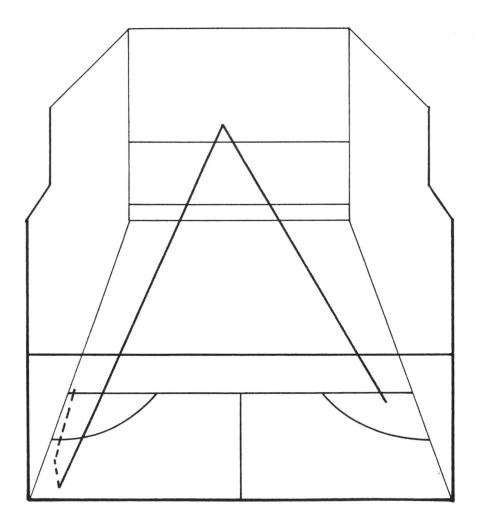

3. *To the T*. The hard serve to the T is aimed at a spot on the front wall approximately one foot from the side wall and just above the service line. After striking this spot the ball rebounds quickly to the side wall, where it gains side spin, and then bounces in the receiver's court close to the T. The receiver is wise to volley the serve, because the ball, after bouncing at the T, jumps quickly to the back wall where it is almost impossible to return.

The hard serve to the T is probably the most difficult of the hard serves to return due to the speed and unusual angle at which the ball travels. In fact, if the serve is executed well, the receiver may miss the shot completely. Unfortunately, the serve is hard to hit with consistent accuracy, and thus a serve which is safer but easier to return must often be used to avoid double faulting.

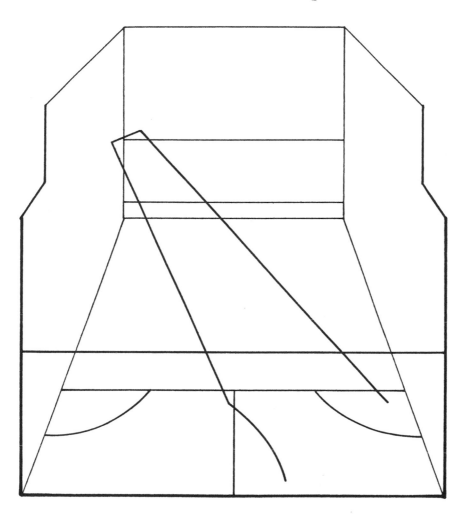

HARD SERVE PRESWING POSITION

1. *Stance and Racket Postion.* For the purpose of deception, the player assumes the same stance and racket position for the hard serve as for the lob, the single exception being that the stance is more closed in the hard serve than in the lob.

2. *Judgment.* After taking the proper preswing position and seeing that his opponent is ready, the player checks the ideal spot on the front wall that will produce the type of hard serve desired. He then looks back at the ball as he prepares to toss it to begin the swing.

3. *Toss of the Ball.* He throws the ball above and a little in front of his right shoulder. The ball must be tossed high enough so that the body and the arm are completely extended when contact is made.

FORESWING

4. *Arm Movement*. As the player tosses the ball, he simultaneously brings the racket back over his right shoulder. The elbow points to the front wall, the wrist is cocked and almost touches the right shoulder, and the racket points to the bottom of the back wall. From this position the player swings, driving his right shoulder and elbow toward the front wall. The body and arm extend upward and slightly forward in a motion much like throwing the racket at the ball. When the arm is almost extended, the wrist snaps quickly so that the ball is hit flat, without spin.

The player must be certain to shift his weight forward during the stroke and to watch the ball closely until it has been hit.

5. *Follow-Through*. In the hard serve, the wrist moves far past the point of impact until the racket head is beyond the left knee. The player then prepares quickly for his opponent's possible return.

Immediate movement to the T is often impossible after hitting a hard serve, especially if the ball is aimed right at the opponent or if the ball strikes the floor first before hitting the back wall.

SLICE SERVE

In the slice serve, the ball is struck at approximately shoulder level in such a way that it gains much sidespin and underspin. The ball travels to a spot on the front wall just above the service line, hits the side wall in the receiver's court just above the floor, and then, because of its spin, dies in the back court.

Like the hard serve, the slice is usually employed as a variation from the lob. But unlike the hard serve, the slice can be a reasonably safe serve, which most opponents have difficulty returning for a winner due to its strange spin and angle. Thus many players use the slice as their basic serve when, for example, the ceiling of the court is very low. But again, surprise is an important part of the effectiveness of the shot and thus the slice is best used sparingly.

SLICE SERVE PRESWING POSITION

1. *Stance and Racket Position.* For the sake of deception, the stance and the initial racket position are the same for the slice as for the hard serve. Deception is important here, since this serve is used to confront the opponent with a change of pace and a lower, flatter trajectory that will cause him to miss or to execute his return ineffectively.

2. *Judgment.* Hit from the right side, the slice serve should strike the front wall just above the service line and slightly left of center. Hit from the left side, the slice serve should strike the front wall at the same height and slightly right of center. The player checks the proper spot after assuming the preswing position and seeing that his opponent is ready. He then looks back at the ball and begins the swing.

3. *Toss of the Ball.* Again, the player throws the ball above and a little in front of his right shoulder, though only just above his head.

FORESWING

4. *Arm Movement.* As he tosses the ball, he brings the racket back to the side. The elbow is out from the body so that the ball can be hit with sidespin, the forearm is parallel to the floor, and the wrist is cocked. As the ball begins its descent, the player snaps his wrist quickly, striking the ball at approximately shoulder level. The open racket face travels from right to left and makes contact with the bottom right quadrant of the ball, giving it both sidespin and underspin.

In the slice serve, as in the hard serve, the player must shift his weight forward from the back leg to the front leg and must watch the ball until contact is made.

5. *Follow-Through.* In the follow-through for the slice serve, the wrist moves through the ball and on toward the front wall. Because of the sideward swing of the racket, however, the wrist and racket are forced to travel in a circular motion until they are pointing to the left side wall at the end of the follow-through. The player then goes quickly to the T and assumes the proper ready position.

COMMON SERVE ERRORS

Lob

1. Rushing the serve—failure to set the feet and the racket properly before hitting

Incorrect   Correct

2. Failure to hit under the ball

Incorrect   Correct

Hard
> Using so big a swing that no explosiveness is possible

Correct

Incorrect

Slice
> Failure to snap the wrist enough to provide the proper spin to the ball

RETURN OF SERVE

In the return of serve, the receiver must realize that he will probably have to hit his shot from deep in the back court and that his opponent probably will be well positioned on the T. Thus the receiver is usually unwise to attempt a winner on the return of serve. Instead, his purpose should almost always be to hit for depth so that he can take the T from his opponent.

Such a purpose is not easy to fulfill, especially since the server has the time to hit with maximum power or control. In fact, if the server is good, the receiver is in danger of losing the point right on the serve. Thus the return of serve must always be hit with great control if the receiver is to prevent outright loss of the point and gain the T position. Since, according to stroke theory, a control shot is best achieved when the player has taken the preswing position early and when there are few body movements, the receiver should await all serves in an alert ready position: facing the side wall, racket back, and knees bent. He should also employ a short foreswing.

Because a major part of the effectiveness of the hard serve is the speed and surprise factor, the receiver should assume that all serves will be hard. He should take his ready position approximately 4 feet from the back wall, with his heels resting on the center line. If the serve is a lob or a slice, he can easily move into position to make a return. But regardless of which serve the opponent uses, the method of return is the same; except under special circumstances, the receiver should return the serve by using the volley.

RETURNING LOB SERVE

Effective volleying of the lob serve is a difficult process demanding excellent control. The shot requires that the receiver contend with two walls, that he redirect the ball from a vertical to a horizontal path, and that he hit the ball so that the opponent is forced to move to the back court to make his return. As a result many players shy away from this volley, but it is a grave mistake to do so; a lob serve which is not volleyed and which bounces on the floor before hitting the back wall is almost impossible to return. The receiver should let the ball bounce only when he is certain that the serve will hit the back wall before hitting the floor. And even then, he must be prepared to make a desperate flip shot from deep in the back corner if he has misjudged the ball.

MOVEMENTS TO RETURN OF LOB PRESWING POSITION

1. *Face Side Wall.* The receiver faces the side wall, back foot approximately four feet from the back wall, heels resting on the center line, as he awaits his opponent's serve. In preparation for a possible hard serve, the receiver is low and in a crouch. He straightens up, however, when his opponent hits the lob serve.

2. *Take Racket Back Early.* As the receiver straightens to take the lob serve, he brings the wrist up to shoulder level. The elbow is held close to the body for extra control while the wrist is cocked.

The racket points to the top of the back wall.

3. *Judgment-Footwork.* As in the ground strokes, quick and proper judgment of the ball's trajectory is essential in the return of the lob serve. The judgment process is made more difficult in returning the lob because the player must take into account the change of direction the ball undergoes when it hits the side wall. The judgment-footwork process begins as soon as the serve is hit with the player constantly watching the ball and

Backhand

Forehand

moving closer to the side wall to make his return. He should position himself underneath the arc of the ball so he can swing in a vertical plane to meet the descending ball. Since maximum control is required in the shot, the player should move quickly so that he is ready to hit before the ball has arrived.

Ideally the receiver should volley the serve about two feet above the shoulders and well out in front of the body. When the player has moved to what he believes to be the spot that will allow him to volley the ball in this manner, he sets his feet in a square stance.

If it is apparent that the ball will definitely hit the back wall before the floor, the receiver should let the ball bounce so that he may hit an easy put-away from center court. Under these conditions, he positions himself near the T as he waits to execute his swing. After swinging he is careful to move out of the path of his opponent so as not to hinder him.

FORESWING

4. *Weight-Shift Forward.* Because the ball must be taken above the head in returning the lob serve, the receiver bends his knees only slightly. Thus weight-shift here is not as pronounced as in the ground strokes. However, it is important that the receiver lean into the ball during the swing, as this does help improve control.

5. *Arm Movement.* As the body moves into the ball, the wrist, cocked perpendicular to the forearm, snaps forward quickly. The swing should not be a big one, because this excess movement is detrimental to control. Contrary to the horizontal swing of the normal volley, the swing of the return of the lob travels over a vertical plane. This way

Backhand

Forehand

the player has the greatest chance of hitting the ball, which is traveling in an almost vertical trajectory.

6. *Follow-Through.* At the end of the follow-through in the return of the lob serve, the racket should point to the top of the front wall. If the serve has been hit poorly, the receiver may go for a winner by aiming just a few inches above the tell-tale. However, it is usually wiser for the player to aim his return at the service line on the front wall close to the side wall so that it goes deep along the side wall. This return forces the server to leave the T to retrieve the shot, allowing the receiver to take the center-court position and so control the play.

RETURNING HARD SERVE

The hard serve, like all other serves, should be volleyed, since this catches the server off-guard and in a weak position on one side of the court. Because of the speed of most hard serves, it is imperative that the receiver accomplish as many preswing movements as possible before the serve is actually hit. Thus the receiver should await the serve facing the side wall with his knees bent, his weight on the balls of his feet, his racket back, and his wrist cocked. Possibly most important, the receiver should be relaxed, as this enables greater quickness and better control.

A powerful return is both unnecessary and unwise. Since the opponent is off-balance after making a hard serve, a powerful return is not needed to defeat him. In addition, because a hard serve allows the player little time for the return, any attempt to hit the ball hard will result in a decrease of control and a high chance of error. To achieve the high degree of control needed to return the hard serve, the player must keep his wrist firmly locked during the swing. The necessary power for the return is furnished by the speed of the serve.

For hard serves hit at him or at his back corner, the receiver should aim his return for a spot approximately three feet above the tell-tale, close to the side wall on his side of the court. Because the server is off-balance after serving, the receiver need not aim too close to the tell-tale to hit an effective return. Indeed, such attempts at pinpoint accuracy often result in the shot's hitting the tin. The key to returning these hard serves is in attacking the ball, not in aiming it an inch above the tin.

For hard serves aimed at the T, the receiver is wise to be safe and hit deep to his own back corner.

Player awaits his opponent's serve in alert ready position.

From return of serve ready position, player steps forward with his front foot and begins to bring racket face forward to ball.

Player continues his swing with his wrist locked, his body forward, and his eyes sharply focused on ball.

Continuing his forward lean, player contacts ball with racket face tilted slightly backward to send ball deep.

Player follows through, racket pointing to front wall and racket face still tilted back.

RETURNING SLICE SERVE

Again, because of the value of the attack, the player should volley when returning the slice serve. The slice serve is difficult to return for a winner, so the receiver should hit deep—either along the side wall or cross-court—so that he may take the all-important T position. Since more power is needed to bring the ball deep, and since the slice serve is not hit as fast as the hard serve, the receiver should add a lot of wrist-snap to the volley stroke in returning the slice serve.

Player awaits his opponent's serve in alert ready position.

Upon determining that serve is a slice, player moves quickly to position himself behind oncoming ball.

Before ball strikes side wall or floor, player "throws" his racket forward and snaps his wrist so as to meet ball in front of his body.

With knees bent deeply and racket face tilted back at a slight angle, player hits deep alley shot.

Player follows through with racket pointing to front wall and body still in a crouch.

COMMON RETURN-OF-SERVE ERRORS

Lob

    1. Failure to use a vertically planed swing to meet the ball

Incorrect   Correct

    2. Using too big a swing

Incorrect   Correct

3. Falling backward when making the foreswing instead of hitting the ball out in front of the body

Incorrect   Correct

Hard

   1. Improper ready position

Incorrect   Correct

2. Judging the flight of the ball slowly and inaccurately

Incorrect

Correct

3. Allowing the ball to strike the back wall instead of volleying it

Incorrect   Correct

Slice
Failure to attack the serve

Incorrect   Correct

SHOTMAKING PLUS MOBILITY

In squash, as in all racket sports, each player must be able to cover a certain court area in a certain amount of time. The player accomplishes this through a systematic use of his mobility and shot-making ability, the combination of which are the actual shots he employs. Because neither player controls the vital T position at the beginning of a point, neither has any advantage as yet. However, as soon as the first shot is made, one player is automatically put at a slight disadvantage. This situation fluctuates between the combatants until one player, due to his superior shots, succeeds in forcing his opponent so far out of position that his ability to cover the necessary court area is drastically reduced. The player is then said to have gained the offensive advantage in the point. His opponent, on the other hand, is said to be on the defensive. In this situation, the player with the offensive advantage attempts to hit shots that will give him the decisive advantage, that is, the point, while the player on the defensive seeks to hit shots that will prevent his opponent from gaining the decisive advantage and that will restore the former equilibrium.

Because the squash court is longer than it is wide, the most effective way of achieving the decisive advantage is to hit shots that move the opponent lengthwise, from back to front to back again.

The two sets of shots that accomplish this task are referred to as the "deep game" and the "short game." The use of the deep game, or, more exactly, the employment of effective passing shots which force the opponent into the back court and cause him to make errors, is the first and most necessary condition for gaining the decisive advantage. The use of the short game, or, more specifically, the employment of those short shots which are either outright winners or take the opponent so far out of position that the player can execute the deep winner, is the necessary complement to the deep game.

DEEP GAME

The deep game consists of all those shots which are designed (1) to move the opponent off the T and into the back court and (2) to gain the decisive advantage should the opponent be caught too far out of position. In its basic form, the deep game consists of a *struggle for the T* in which each player uses the shots of the deep game to drive the opponent into the back court, where the slightest error will give the player a strong offensive advantage. A second form the deep game may take is what can be called the *offensive deep game*. In this case, the player, having gained the offensive advantage either by moving his opponent to the forecourt or by trapping him along one side wall, uses one of the shots of the deep game as a putaway. The final form the deep game may take can be called the *defensive deep game,* and it is used in direct response to the offensive deep game by the player who has been forced far out of position.

The deep game is comprised of only three shots: the alley, the cross-court, and the lob. However, each shot is executed in a slightly different way, depending on whether the player uses it in the struggle for the T, in the offensive deep game, or in the defensive deep game.

The alley, a shot which travels to and from the front wall along one side wall, is used only in the struggle for the T and in the offensive deep game. When the shot is used to gain the T, it should be aimed 3 to 5 feet above the tin so that it goes deep to the back court; when it is hit for a winner, the shot should be aimed approximately 3 to 6 inches above the tin so that it dies quickly. In both cases the alley is executed with the standard stroke, discussed earlier in the sections on stroke theory and stroke application.

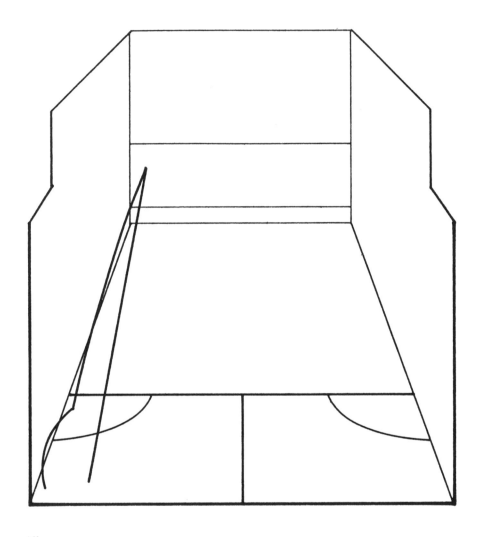

Alley

The cross-court travels from one side of the court to approximately the middle of the front wall and finally to the other side of the court, where it strikes the side wall just above the horizontal T line. Again, this shot is used only in the battle for the T and in the offensive deep game. A player employing a deep cross-court must be careful in his aim; a cross-court which hits too low on the front wall can be half-volleyed for a winner by the opponent on the T while a cross-court which hits too high on the front wall comes out to the center of the court and can be put away with an offensive alley shot. The exact spot on the front wall where the ball should strike for the deep cross-court varies depending upon the speed at which the shot is hit. But generally, the ball should not hit the front wall lower than 3 feet or higher than 4 feet above the tin. An offensive cross-court is not as difficult to execute successfully as the deep cross-court and should be aimed about 3 to 6 inches above the tin. Like the alley, the cross-court is made with the standard stroke. The only difference in stroke execution for the two shots is that the wrist is snapped earlier for the cross-court than the alley.

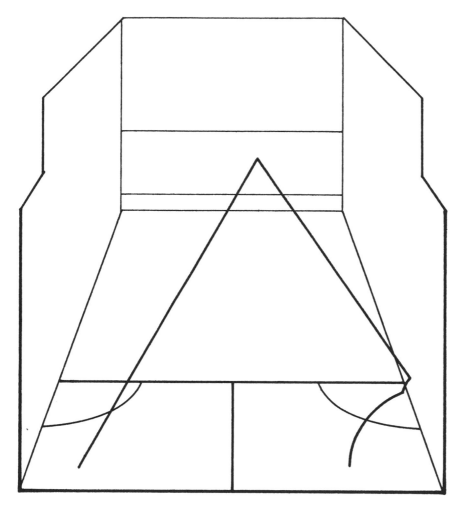

Cross-Court

The lob is a highly arched shot that hits well up on the front wall and lands deep in the back court. It is often employed in the struggle for the T when an opponent is particularly tenacious at holding center court. The lob is also the only shot in the defensive deep game, because it is the only shot which allows the player who is far out of position to return to the T before his opponent makes his next shot. On the other hand, the lob is seldom if ever used by a player with the offensive advantage because the shot normally enables the opponent on the defensive to get back into position.

When the lob is employed to move the opponent off the T, it can be hit along either the wall or cross-court depending on which way the opponent on the T is leaning. It can be hit either with top-spin or with backspin, as the player prefers. In either case, the stroke is the same as that used for the ground strokes except that the wrist is kept firm and the follow-through ends high. When used defensively, the lob should be hit only along the alley, since this is the easiest lob to execute while running at top speed. Because the player has so little time to make the defensive alley lob, he must use a special, highly controlled stroke in which all the power for the shot is furnished by a quick snap of the wrist. A more precise explanation of this special stroke will be given later.

While the preceding comments give some idea of the shots comprising the deep game, these descriptions are by no means complete, for they do not explain how the shots of the deep game are employed in a match situation. Let us turn to a common example of each of the three forms of the deep game to see how shotmaking and mobility combine in actual play.

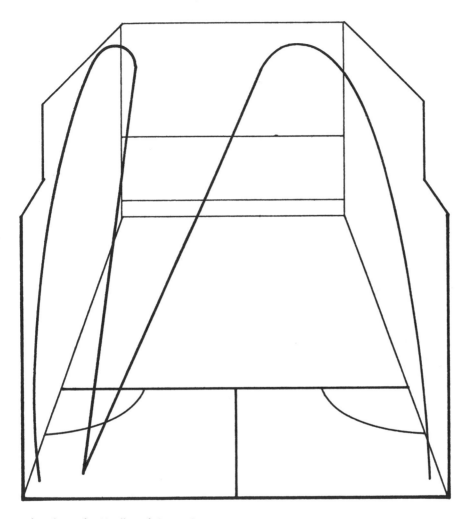

Lob, Along the Wall and Cross-Court

THE STRUGGLE FOR THE T

1. *Ready Position on the T*

Situation: The player stands on the T in the ready position while his opponent hits from deep in the back court. The opponent executes a deep passing shot, close to the right side wall. The player judges the flight of the ball quickly and decides that it will be too difficult a shot to volley but that it will come off the back wall. Thus he decides to move to the back court to take the shot.

Player begins movement to ball.

2. *Movement to the Preswing Position*

Situation: The player now has free passage to retrieve the ball:

a. The player turns to face the side wall, and simultaneously takes his racket back.

b. He judges the speed and height of the ball to determine how far the ball will come out from the back wall and moves to the back corner rapidly.

Important points: The player must move quickly enough to be in good position when the ball arrives. He must also be sure to go deep enough to avoid having to fall back and reach behind his body to hit the ball, though not so deep that his swing is cramped by the back wall.

c. As he reaches the spot on the court that he judges to be correct, the player sets his feet in the closed stance.

Proper preswing position near back wall, racket back.

3. *Foreswing*

Situation: The player stands deep in the back court, having exchanged position with his opponent. A winner is difficult to make from the back court, especially when the opponent holds the T position. In fact, such an attempt usually results in the player's losing the point outright. Thus, the player's purpose here is to force his opponent to the back court so that he (the player) can retake the T. The player may use any one of three shots to accomplish his purpose— the deep alley, the deep cross-court, or the lob. Because his opponent is well stationed on the T, the player decides to hit the deep alley, because this shot is most effective at pulling the opponent off the T *and* at forcing him to hit from a weak position:

The player takes a small step forward with his front foot and simultaneously swings the racket into and through the ball.

Important points: The player must be certain to shift his weight forward into the ball, since this action gives the shot force and ultimately causes the ball to die in the back court. Proper timing of the swing is also crucial. Contrary to every other shotmaking situation in which the ball moves toward the racket, taking the ball after it comes off the back wall is a shotmaking situation in which the racket and the ball move in the same direction. Also, the ball often rises above the waist after it has bounced on the floor and then hit the back wall. Both of these conditions require special timing of the stroke, whereby the player waits until the ball has come down to knee level before he begins the foreswing. When play is fast, such patience is difficult; the player is often tense and tends to want to hit quickly so that he can move back to the T. Yet the player who forces himself to wait for the ball to drop hits with a more pronounced knee-bend, and thus increases the power, control, and deception of his shot.

As the player swings, he should give the ball a little sidespin, drawing the strings of the racket slightly from right to left so that the ball hugs the side wall on its return. The player also should aim for a spot that is high enough on the front wall to ensure that the ball makes its first bounce near the floor service line. Both of these precautions make the shot more difficult for the opponent to volley.

As ball drops low, player leans forward and swings with slight sidespin.

4. Movement Back to the T

Situation: The player moves back to the T position while his opponent, having the right of way, attempts to retrieve the ball.

Having hit the alley, the player, under normal circumstances, must move around behind his opponent to reach the newly vacated center-court area. However, if the player has executed his deep alley shot close to the crossing line of the T, and/or if the opponent is one who readily allows himself to be diverted from his preferred path to the ball, the player should "move through" the ball and take the T by going in front of his opponent. The advantage of this forward movement is threefold: (a) it allows the player to reach the T more quickly than usual; (b) it ensures that the player will hit a more powerful, more controlled, and more aggressive shot; and (c) it steals some of the valuable time the opponent needs to reach the shot. It must be remembered, however, that the opponent does have the right of way and would be justified in calling a let if obstructed in any way in his movement to the ball. In this particular situation, let us assume that forward movement to the T is not possible, and that therefore the player has had to travel behind his opponent. Of course, if the player had hit cross-court instead of down the side wall, he would have been able to move directly back to the T with no possibility of the opponent's calling a let.

Important point: Regardless of which shot the player uses to dislodge his opponent from center court, he must get to the T as quickly as possible, especially if his opponent likes the volley. Even if the player is only one step from the T when his opponent hits the ball, he will probably lose the point.

Player quickly moves behind opponent to the T.

5. *Ready Position on the T*

Situation: Once again, the player stands on the T and alertly awaits his opponent's return.

The procedure for the proper execution of the offensive deep game is very similar to the procedure just discussed. However, some differences in execution and movement do exist and should be explained more fully.

Player reassumes ready position and carefully watches his opponent.

OFFENSIVE DEEP GAME—DEEP PUTAWAY

The offensive deep game situation usually arises when the player catches his opponent out of position in the front court. In this case, the preferred shot is a low alley hit with moderate speed. The most important requirement in making any offensive deep shot is that the elbow be kept close to the body. Any hitch in the stroke is unnecessary and only results in the ball's going too deep, allowing the opponent to reach it as it rebounds off the back wall.

Deep putaway with opponent in front court.

The offensive deep game situation is also brought about when the opponent hits a deep cross-court too high or too hard. The result is that the ball comes out too far from the back wall and traps the opponent along the side wall. The offensive deep shot in this situation is more difficult to execute. Again the preferred shot is the low alley (though the low cross-court which catches the opponent going the wrong way should be used occasionally as a deceptive variation). However, in this case, the player is positioned a little behind the T and so must aim a little higher on the front wall, about 6 inches above the tin, to be sure to avoid error. Again the elbow should be held close to the body during the stroke.

Deep putaway with opponent close to side wall.

With his opponent trapped along side wall, player backs up quickly in crouch position and executes deep putaway shot.

When making the offensive deep shot in either of these situations, the player must be certain to move to the hitting position quickly. In the first case, the opponent usually has hit a low, fast shot from the front court. Thus while the player has a strong offensive advantage with his opponent close to the front wall, he can easily lose the point if he is not well prepared to cut off his opponent's shot. In the second case, the opponent has hit a cross-court which has rebounded from the back wall directly at the player and is moving at a rapid pace. The player must move back quickly and stay low or he will be forced to hit the ball too close to his body and may commit an error. He also must be certain to keep his hitting elbow close to his body throughout the swing, since a hitch in the swing usually results in the ball's striking the tin.

INCORRECT EXECUTION OF OFFENSIVE DEEP SHOT

Player failing to back up quickly enough to allow his knees to be bent and his hips to be low.

Player improperly adding hitch in the elbow when beginning his foreswing.

DEFENSIVE DEEP GAME—STOPPING DEEP PUTAWAY

1. *Ready Position Near the Side Wall*

Situation: We shall assume that the player has hit a deep cross-court with too much power so that he is now trapped along the side wall by the opponent who is backing up to take the shot. The opponent, having the offensive advantage, attempts a deep putaway shot from center court. Unless there is some indication to the contrary, the player must assume that his opponent will hit the percentage shot which is in the hard, low alley. In this case, the player must run across the court to the other side wall, a relatively great distance, in a short amount of time. Thus, to maximize his quickness, he must accomplish as many preswing movements as possible before his opponent hits:

a. The player assumes a crouched position, alert but relaxed, with his racket arm extended slightly forward, his shoulders down and his knees bent.

Important point: Each of these movements should be accomplished with the player facing the opposite side wall, a tactic which allows him to run most quickly across the court.

b. The player positions himself as close to the center as possible without having to step back at the last instant to avoid his opponent's swing.

Important point: In assuming the ready position, the player must watch his opponent's wrist and racket face very carefully in order to determine whether the ball will go down the alley or cross-court. If the opponent chooses not to hit the percentage alley and if the player fails to notice the indications in the opponent's stroke that the cross-court is to be made, the player will be caught going the wrong way.

Player anticipates opponent's deep putaway facing side wall with wrist cocked and knees bent.

2. *Movement to the Ball*

Situation: The player must run at top speed to reach his opponent's alley shot:

a. From a relaxed ready position, the player explodes off the mark once his opponent has hit.

b. However, while the player's start is explosive, his movement is smooth. He retrieves the shot by taking a few low, fast, gliding steps, the soles of the feet rising just above the floor.

In a low glide, player moves quickly to retrieve ball; wrist remains cocked.

3. Foreswing

Situation: The player, moving rapidly, must hit from a bad position in the court. His purpose, then, is to retrieve his opponent's shot and to return it in such a way that he (the player) will have time to move back to the T. The only shot available to the player in this situation is the alley lob, hit with the highest possible control:

a. When the player sees that his opponent's shot is just about to die, he takes a giant, lunging step with the right foot. This long step gives the player maximum reach, allowing him to return more difficult shots with less chance of the ball's striking the side wall during its flight.

b. At the same time, the player snaps his wrist hard, hitting under the ball as much as possible in order to send it high up on the front wall. For maximum control, this snapping of the wrist must be the only arm movement in the swing.

Player snaps his wrist and lobs ball along side wall.

4. *Movement Back to the T*

Situation: As the opponent retrieves the alley lob, the player returns to the T:

Again, the opponent has the right of way, and thus the player must circle behind the opponent in order to move back to the center.

Important point: The player must return to the T quickly, since the opponent will attack for a winner if the lob is not very accurate.

While watching ball, player moves low to the T.

5. *Ready Position on the T*

Situation: The player assumes the ready position on the T, having restored the equilibrium between himself and his opponent.

Ready position on the T.

SHORT GAME

The short game consists of all those shots which are designed (1) to move the opponent into the front court and out of position and (2) to gain the decisive advantage if possible. The short game may take two forms, *offensive* and *defensive*. The offensive short game is the complement of the deep game and is employed when the player is in good position in midcourt and his opponent is in the back court. In this situation, the player may hit a soft shot, or what is also referred to as a touch shot, in order to win the point outright or simply to gain an even stronger offensive advantage by moving his opponent farther out of position. The defensive short game is always used when the player must lunge desperately in order to reach his opponent's touch shot which is about to die in the front court.

The short game consists primarily of four shots: the drop, the reverse drop, the corner, and the reverse corner. As in the case of the deep game, the shots comprising the short game are hit differently, depending on whether they are used offensively or defensively.

The drop is an alley shot that, ideally, nicks on the crack between the side wall and the floor near the front wall. It is hit softly but crisply and, when employed offensively, is executed with a little side-spin as well. When used defensively, the drop is made with a slight flip of the wrist (to be explained in more detail later), and is the only short shot employed in the defensive short game. The drop should be aimed at a spot on the front wall a few inches above the tin and about a foot from the side wall.

Drop

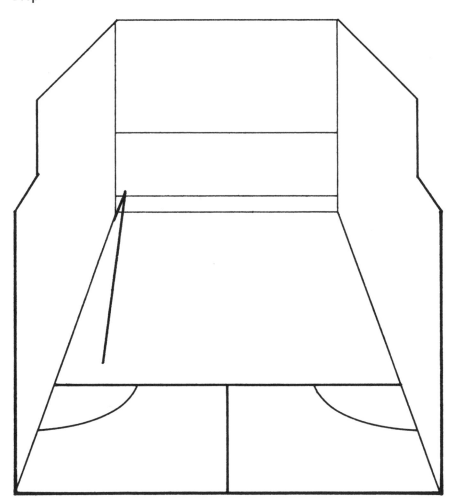

The reverse drop is a cross-court drop shot in which again the ball is hit softly but crisply and with a little sidespin. The reverse drop should be aimed a few inches above the tin, though not quite as close to the side wall as the drop.

Reverse Drop

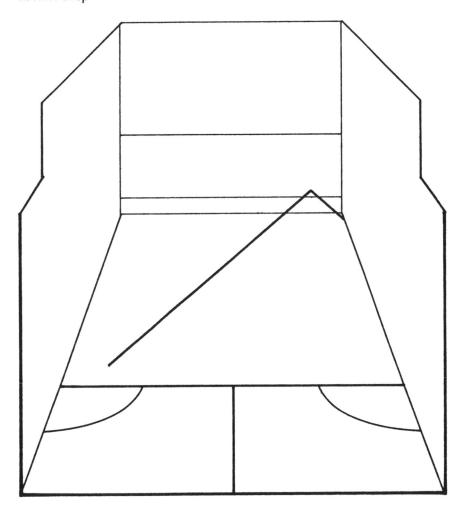

The corner is a shot in which the ball strikes the side wall to-ward which the player is facing and then rebounds to the front wall. The ball should hit the side wall a few feet from the front wall and should strike the front wall about three inches above the tell-tale line. The shot should be executed sharply so that the ball dies quickly. However, the player must be careful not to hit the ball so hard that it reaches the other side wall before it has bounced twice.

Corner

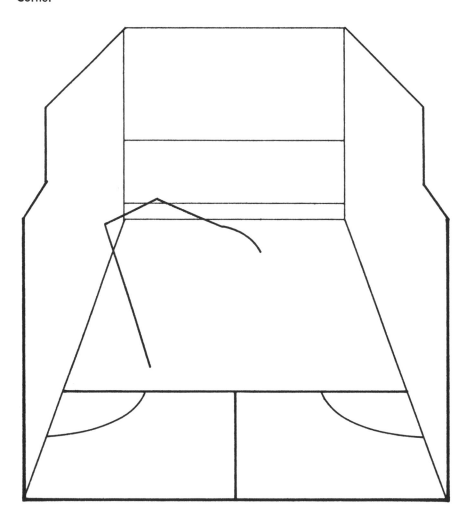

The reverse corner is a shot in which the ball travels cross-court to the opposite side wall and then, like the corner, strikes the front wall approximately three inches above the tin. Because of the position of the player in the court, the ball should hit the side wall closer to the front wall on the reverse corner than on the corner. Again, the shot should be executed sharply but without so much force that the ball fails to bounce a second time before striking the other side wall.

Reverse Corner

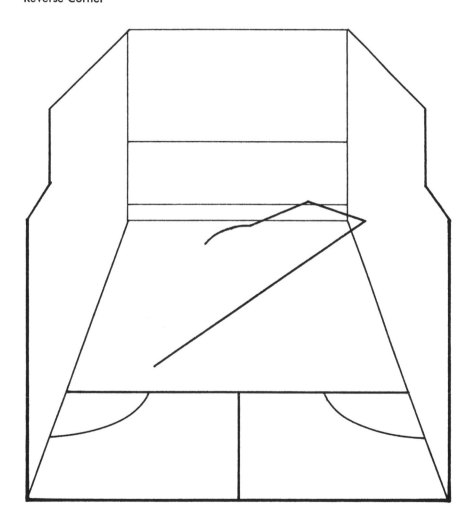

Two other shots, not usually considered part of the short game, should be mentioned here. The "3-wall" and the roll corner are both shots which are hit from the back court and which appear to the opponent to be deep shots. However, both drop in the front court and are always intended to end the point. In the 3-wall shot, the ball is aimed at a sharp angle into the facing side wall with the ideal result that the ball strikes the front wall just above the tin and a few feet from the opposite side wall, and then nicks on the crack between that side wall and the floor. The stroke for the 3-wall shot is similar to that for a deep passing shot, with one important difference: In executing the foreswing for the 3-wall shot, the wrist must be kept firm and unbroken. The shot is best hit at three-quarters speed.

"3-Wall"

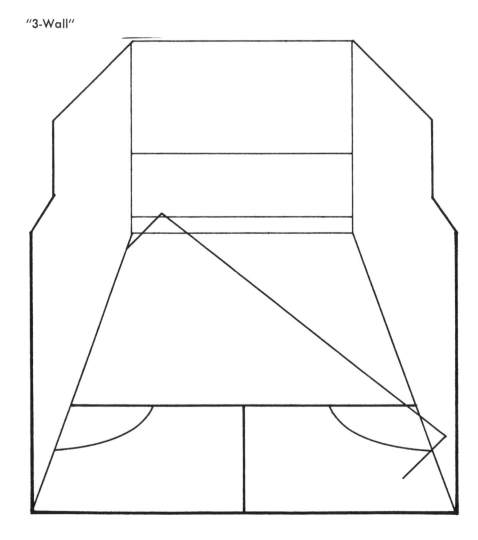

The roll corner, executed from the back court, is merely a long corner shot, which strikes the side wall about five feet from the front wall, rebounds to the front wall about six inches above the tin, and then dies in the front court near the opposite side wall. Again, the stroke here is virtually the same as that used for any passing shot except that the foreswing is slower and employs less of a snap in the wrist. The 3-wall shot and the roll corner are by no means easy shots, but neither are they very risky if used in the right situation (to be discussed more fully in the section on tactics).

For both the offensive and defensive short game, the player must use a special stroke when executing his shot, and these are best explained within the context of a match situation. Let us then take a look at a common example of the two kinds of short game.

Roll Corner

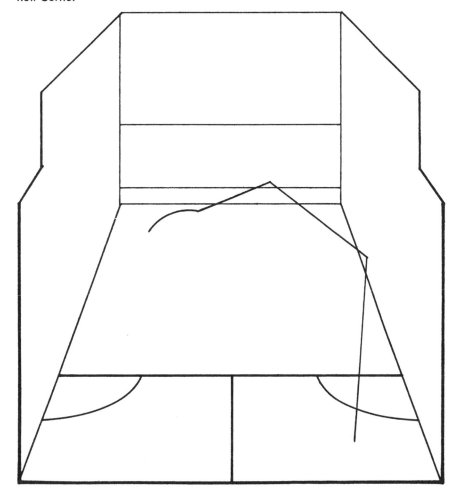

OFFENSIVE SHORT GAME—SHORT PUTAWAY

1. *Ready Position on the T*

Situation: The player stands on the T in the ready position while his opponent executes a shot from the back court. Let us assume that the opponent, in the right corner of the back court, tries a deep alley shot, but the ball hits too low on the front wall and then grazes the side wall during its flight. The ball bounces in midcourt a few feet in front of the T, allowing the player to attack for the winner.

Player judges flight of ball.

2. *Movement to the Preswing Position*

Situation: The player has free passage to the ball, but he must move quickly in order to execute his shot correctly:

a. The player judges the flight of the ball so that he may rapidly and accurately move to the ideal hitting position to make his shot.

Important point: Retrieving a shot which bounces in front of the player is the one example in squash in which the player does not turn sideways and take his racket back first but rather runs immediately to the shot, racket in front of the body. This enables the player to move with maximum quickness if the ball is just about to bounce a second time and to turn sideways and take the racket back for maximum control and deception if he has more time.

b. The present shot requires no forward movement by the player, so he turns to face the right side wall and simultaneously takes the racket back.

Important point: For the purpose of deception, the racket is held behind the body in the same position as that used for hard shots. In this way, the player hits the short shot off the same stroke as for the deep shot.

c. Since the ideal spot to hit the ball is at knee level, the player bends his knees deeply to allow his wrist to be lower than the racket head.

Important point: To ensure maximum control, this knee-bend (and weight-shift) must occur before the foreswing begins so that there is no excess movement during the swing.

Player is low and his racket is back.

3. *Foreswing*

Situation: The player has a strong offensive advantage and thus his purpose is to attack for a winner. The player can use any one of a number of shots, including the drop, the reverse drop, the corner, and the reverse corner to achieve his purpose. He decides to hit a drop shot for the winner:

a. So that the shot will be most deceptive, the player begins the foreswing for the soft shot as if he were hitting hard. The right shoulder drops lower than the left, the elbow drives forward, and the wrist remains cocked.

b. To keep control high, the player attempts to remove as many movements as possible from the swing without decreasing deception. He does not snap his wrist when executing the drop shot, but instead, uses a slight scooping stroke in which he meets the ball with a flat racket head and then ends the stroke by lifting the bottom half of the racket head. In this way, the player gets maximum face on the ball as he hits, aiding control, but also imparts vital underspin to the shot to make it die quickly. Throughout the entire stroke, the player keeps his elbow close to the body.

Important points: The player should impart a slight sidespin to the ball, which makes it hug the side wall, and he should aim the ball approximately three inches above the tin so that it dies quickly.

Player strikes ball with flat racket face . . .

. . then lifts bottom of racket face and slides it to the left.

4. *Movement Back to the T*

Situation: The opponent has the right-of-way in his movement to retrieve the player's shot:

a. Having made the drop shot, the player moves quickly and directly back to the T once he has hit so that the opponent cannot call a let.

b. If the player had executed a reverse drop, a corner, or a reverse corner, he would have to delay his movement back to the T in order to give the opponent free passage to the ball.

Expecting a return, player backs quickly to take ready position.

5. *Ready Position on the T*

Situation: The player is again in an alert ready position on the T:

a. To be prepared for the opponent's possible return, the player assumes that his opponent will retrieve his shot.

b. The player takes his ready position one step in front of the T and one step to the side of the T in which the opponent will hit his shot. This is because the most effective returns the opponent can make are a drop shot and an alley shot, both of which stay close to the side wall.

Important point: The player must be certain not to go too far forward or too much to one side or he will be open to a cross-court shot by the opponent.

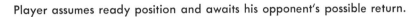

Player assumes ready position and awaits his opponent's possible return.

DEFENSIVE SHORT GAME—STOPPING SHORT PUTAWAY

1. *Ready Position in the Back Court*

Situation: Let us assume that the player has hit a deep alley shot from the back court which has nicked the side wall during its flight. His opponent on the T now has the offensive advantage and can use a number of different shots to gain the decisive advantage:

a. In order to move directly to the opponent's shot and to avoid being caught going the wrong way, the player stops his movement back to the T just before his opponent hits and quickly assumes the ready position.

Before his opponent hits, player takes ready position, no matter where he is standing at the time.

2. *Movement to the Ball*

Situation: Let us further assume that the opponent hits a very accurate drop shot, requiring the player to cover a large area of the court in a relatively short time. The great speed at which the player must run just to reach the ball before it dies demands that the return be hit with total control, because any extra movement could cause the player to miss the ball altogether. Thus, once again, the player must accomplish as many preswing movements as possible before he reaches the ball and must remove all movements from the swing except the wrist-snap:

a. The player, already on the balls of his feet, explodes from a relaxed stance and runs to the ball, using smooth, gliding steps.

b. As he moves to the front wall, he extends his right arm in front of him so that his racket is pointing toward the ball, forehand face up.

   Important point: Hard running makes concentration especially difficult, so the player must be certain to watch the ball closely.

Racket forward, player runs low.

3. *Foreswing*

Situation: The player must hit his shot close to the front wall while running at top speed. His opponent, on the other hand, is well positioned in center court. The player's purpose is to hit a shot which will pull the opponent off the T and allow the player time to return to a better court position:

a. When the opponent's shot is just about to bounce a second time, the player takes a long step and bends deeply so that he can reach under the ball with the racket.

b. Then, using only wrist-snap to provide direction and power to his shot, the player flips the ball to the front wall.

Player reaches under ball and snaps wrist.

If the player feels that his opponent is standing on the T, he should snap his wrist softly and aim the shot so that the ball bounces on the floor close to the side wall after it strikes the front wall. This way the opponent must run hard to the front wall and must contend with the side wall as he makes his return.

Short Flip

If the player senses that his opponent has moved close behind him in expectation of the drop, he should snap his wrist hard and send the ball deep.

Deep Flip

4. *Movement Back to the T*

Situation: The opponent, moving to return the player's shot, has free passage to the ball. If the player has employed the deep flip shot, he can move directly back to the T. If the player has hit the short flip, he must move slightly to the side to allow his opponent to reach the ball. However, this movement must not be too great or the player will take himself out of position and will slow his movement back to center court:

> After executing his shot, the player back-pedals rapidly, moving low with his weight forward and on the balls of his feet. The wrist is cocked and the racket head is up so that the player can volley rapidly if necessary.

> Important point: If possible, the player should stop his backward movement as soon as his opponent begins to make his shot, so that he can run quickly in any direction to retrieve his opponent's possible return. Because of the nature of this situation, the player will probably not have time to get all the way to the T; either the player's shot is an outright winner or his opponent retrieves the shot before the player has completed his backward movement.

While backing to the T, player watches carefully for his opponent's possible return.

SHOTMAKING PRACTICE

The use of shotmaking drills is the fastest way possible to improve one's level of play. Drills, by nature, are highly specialized, allowing a player to work intensively on one area of his game. As a result, a player who is unable to overcome a certain problem in his game through simple match play can often overcome the obstacle quickly and easily by employing the right drill. By the same token, a player can increase the rate at which his general level of play improves by using a series of drills which focus on the important areas of the game.

Of course, each player has his own particular shotmaking characteristics and problems. Understandably, then, each player would benefit most from a drill program that he could adapt to his own particular practice needs. Such a program follows, distilling all exercise possibilities down to four basic types of drills. Each type of exercise displays a progressively higher degree of the important judgment-footwork variable of shotmaking, and each is named according to that aspect of shotmaking that it emphasizes:

1. "Foreswing" Drill: The player faces the side wall, takes a set stance with his racket back, and hits the ball along the alley so that it returns to him.
2. "Racket-back" Drill: The player must take his racket back before making each stroke, but still is not required to move to the ball.
3. "Attack" Drill: The player now attacks the ball and shifts his weight forward, while accomplishing the other swing movements as well.
4. "Combination" Drill: The player must execute all swing motions as well as move to the ball.

Using these and the more particular drills presented below, each player can choose the area and drills he needs. It is suggested, however, that when the player is working on some area of his game he begin with the first type of drill (requiring least judgment-footwork), and then move gradually to each succeeding type. Every player, especially the beginner, must expect that his level of execution will decrease as he adds more movement to his drills. The more advanced players can progress rapidly to the more difficult types of drills; indeed, they are advised to spend most of their drill time on these later types of exercise, since, for advanced players, efficiency of movement is usually the factor which distinguishes the great player from the good one.

Regardless of ability, a player is wise to heed an important warning: Always take the time to participate in a few drills before playing actual games. The player who attempts to practice his shots by playing a large number of games only succeeds in grooving improper strokes as he becomes tired. On the other hand, the player who drills and *then* plays first sharpens his strokes and then imprints them firmly by playing the resulting high-quality match. Of course, for those who play squash only for the excellent exercise it provides, such care in workout procedure is not so important. However, if a player is at all concerned with improving his game as well as staying in shape, he should always follow the procedure of drill-play-exercise.

FOREHAND AND BACKHAND

1. *Foreswing Drill.* Take the preswing position—facing the side wall, racket back, feet in a closed stance—near the side wall a little behind the horizontal line of the T. Then throw the ball against the side wall so that it bounces to the appropriate height and distance from the front knee. Using the proper foreswing technique, hit the ball and aim at a spot on the front wall which will cause the ball to return to approximately that same point opposite the front knee. Return to the preswing position as the ball travels to and from the front wall, and then at the appropriate time, hit the ball again. Repeat this process until you gain proficiency, and then begin again on the other side of the court with the opposite ground stroke.

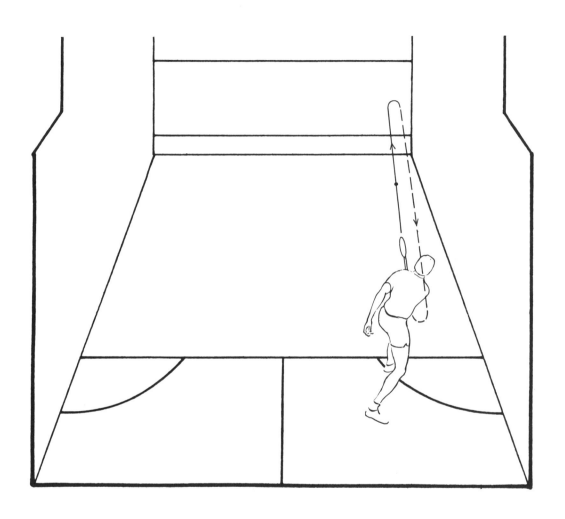

2. *Racket-back Drill.* Stand near the side wall approximately five feet in front of the horizontal T-line, facing the side wall. Using moderate power, hit the ball along the alley. The quickness with which the ball returns to you should force you to get set in the correct preswing position rapidly and efficiently. Of course, the ball should not be struck so hard that you are physically unable to assume this preswing position in time or, worse, so hard that you find yourself leaning or falling back as you make the foreswing.

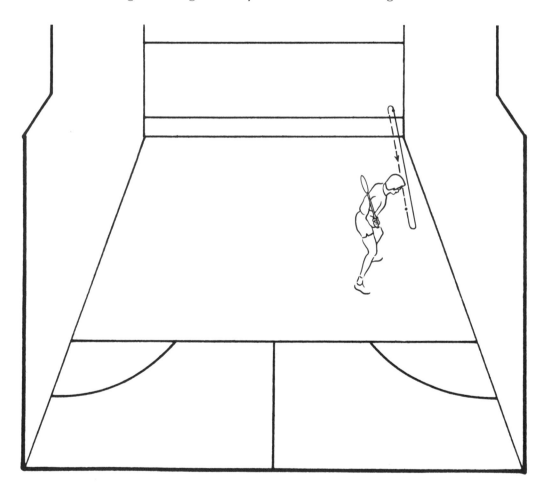

3. *Attack Drill.* Assume the ready position on the T and hit, or preferably have a partner hit to you, a series of low, three-quarters-speed shots. As the ball approaches, step forward and place the racket face behind the oncoming ball. Snap your wrist hard and send the ball low and fast across the court. The stroke is a modified ground stroke tailored for speed, so avoid using any extra motion of the hitting elbow or arm. Moreover, be sure to attack the ball even though it may be moving very fast; stepping into the ball is the only certain way to hit an effective shot every time.

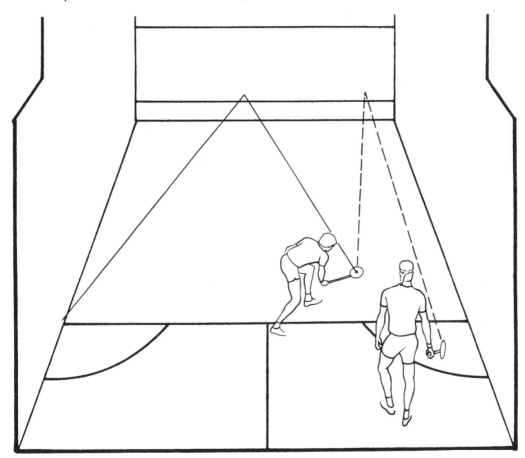

4. *Midcourt-Movement (Combination) Drill.* This exercise is the best all-around drill in squash, and can be used by a player of virtually any ability. To implement the drill, take the ready position on the T and have a partner who is standing in one of the back corners of the court hit a medium-paced shot which bounces a little behind the cross-bar of the T upon its return. After quickly judging the trajectory of the ball, turn sideways, take your racket back all the way, and move rapidly to the proper spot *behind* the shot, so that you are able to *lean into* the ball when you return it. Execute a medium-paced alley shot, return to the T, and prepare yourself to meet your partner's next shot on either side of the court. The primary purpose of the exercise is to integrate mobility with shotmaking, so be certain that all preswing movements are accomplished before the ball arrives.

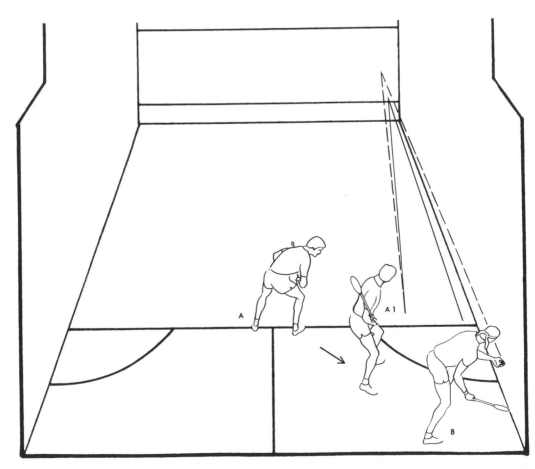

5. *Combination Drill.* Stand midway between the horizontal T-line and the back wall, near a back corner, and, executing properly, hit a cross-court. Aim the ball so that it reaches the ideal hitting position at approximately the identical spot in the opposite back corner. Be sure that you judge the flight of the ball and move very quickly so that you have assumed the proper preswing position before the ball arrives at the other side of the court. Once you have gained this position, execute the correct foreswing, again hitting a cross-court. The purpose of this exercise is to learn quick judgment and footwork, and to practice rapid attainment of the preswing position even while on the run. Therefore, be certain to hit the ball slowly enough at first to allow yourself the necessary time to move to the proper preswing position before the ball arrives. As you become more proficient, increase the speed of the shot.

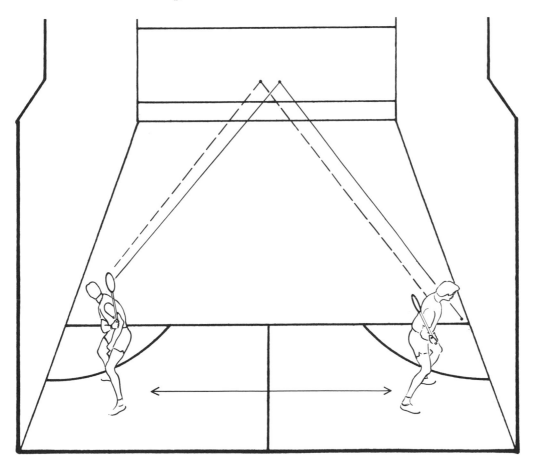

VOLLEY

Because taking the racket back is detrimental to the volley, we include no "foreswing" or "racket-back" drill.

1. *Attack Drill.* Assume the preswing position approximately five feet in front of the horizontal T line and a few feet from one side wall. Aiming for a spot on the front wall which will result in the ball's returning to about shoulder level on the same side of the body it is originally hit, use the proper volley stroke to make the shot. Quickly regain the preswing position (racket *in front of* the hitting shoulder) and repeat the shot. Having executed a sufficient number of volleys on one side of the body, turn and execute an appropriate number on the other side. Primary emphasis should be placed upon attacking the ball, hitting it well out in front of the body.

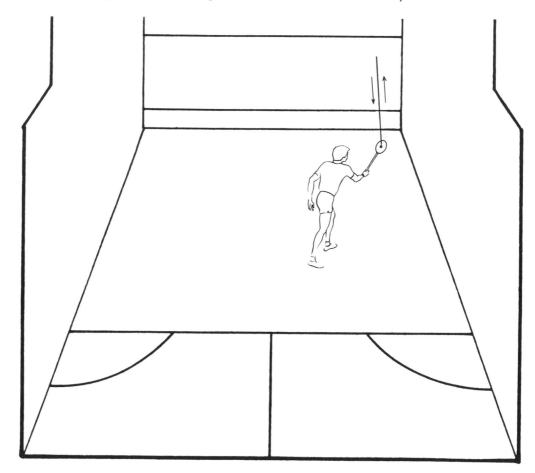

2. *Combination Drill.* Stand at the same distance from the T as in the previous drill but in the center of the court instead of to one side. Then hit the volley cross-court to shoulder level on your other side. In the short time that the ball is traveling, bring the racket back to the ready position, lean forward, and make another cross-court volley. Hit the ball relatively slowly so that with very quick movements you are able to attack the ball on each stroke. To further emphasize movement and timing, advance toward the front wall as you hit. Again primary consideration should be given to hitting the ball far out in front of the body.

In order to practice the half-volley, modify the preceding volley drills so that the ball bounces on the floor in front of you before you execute your shot.

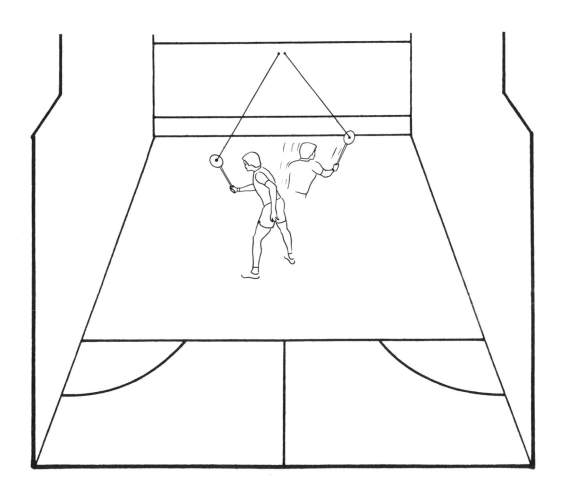

DEEP GAME

1. *Combination Drill (A)*. The purpose of this exercise is to provide a player with an intensive repetition of deep passing shots so that he may groove his deep game and gain the proper rhythm needed for success in this area. To execute the drill, stand near one of the corners of the back court and hit a deep alley shot. Aim higher than usual so that the ball will rebound off the back wall after it has bounced on the floor once. While the ball travels to and from the front wall, quickly judge its flight and then assume the proper pre-swing position before the ball has returned. As the ball comes off the back wall, hesitate until the ball has almost reached the ideal hitting spot at knee level before beginning *any part of* the foreswing, and then hit the deep alley shot again. Be certain of proper foreswing execution. If you find that you are unable to shift your weight forward during the foreswing, it is because you have overestimated the distance of the rebound of the ball from the back wall. To correct this problem, stand closer to the back wall as you wait to make each shot. Emphasis in this drill should be placed upon getting set early and hesitating for a sufficient amount of time for the ball to drop to knee level before beginning the foreswing.

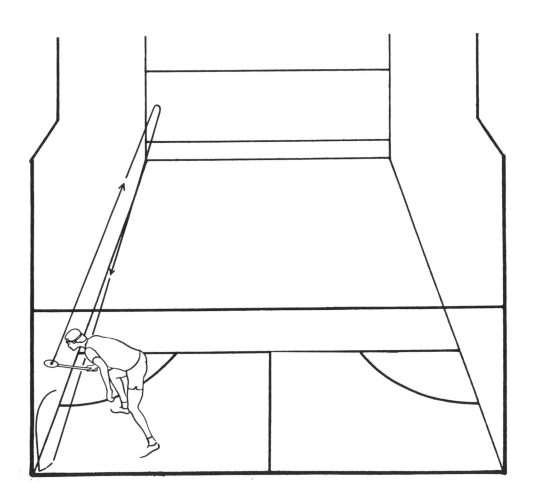

2. *Combination Drill (B)*. With the presence of a second person, the alley drill explained above allows the player to incorporate matchlike movement to and from the T into his deep-game practice. For this exercise, take the ready position on the T and have a partner execute a deep alley shot from one corner of the back court. Switch positions with him and repeat the deep alley shot. For the drill to be effective, the ball should be hit higher on the front wall than would be appropriate in a match so that the ball will rebound off the back wall. This allows you to practice the hesitation needed when returning a deep shot which comes off the back wall.

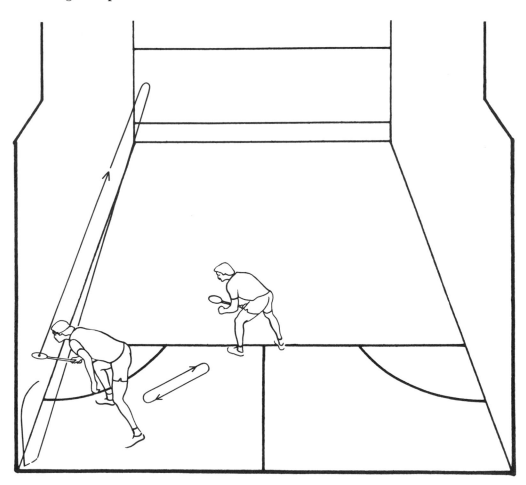

3. *"No Side Wall" Game (Combination Drill)*. This drill is useful for improving both the short and the deep game, but is particularly beneficial to the deep game. With a partner, play a regular game of squash with the exception that neither player is allowed to hit a shot in which the ball strikes the side wall before the front wall. If such a shot is made, whether intentionally or not, the player responsible automatically loses the point. The drill is an excellent one for improving your deep game, because it forces you to move to the ball to get set quicker, in order to prevent making a shot in which the ball hits the side wall first. As a result, you quickly increase your capability of hitting deep passing shots which hug the side wall instead of those which hit the side wall and land in center court for an easy winner for your opponent.

SHORT GAME

1. *Foreswing Drill.* The short game in squash requires a great deal of accuracy, and this exercise, due to its constant repetition of the foreswing, is very helpful. To execute this drill, stand on some spot in front of the T near one side wall and take the preswing position, ball held in the free hand. Throw the ball against the side wall so that it bounces to the proper hitting spot and then hit a drop shot. Try to make the ball nick so that it dies after it hits the side wall. Of course, this drill requires that you pick up the ball and throw it against the side wall for each stroke. To ensure diversity in your short game, be certain to execute other short shots besides the drop shot; also be sure to hit these shots from various places in front of the T.

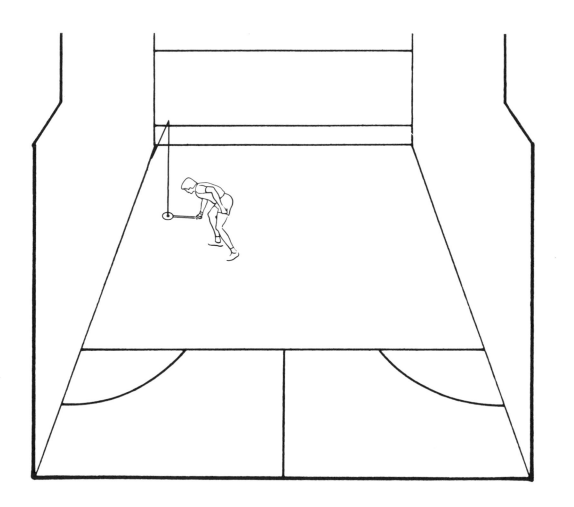

2. *"Cat-and-Mouse"* (*Combination*) *Drill.* Like the "No Side Wall" game, the "Cat-and-Mouse" drill aids both the deep game and the short game. In this case, however, the exercise is more beneficial to the short game. In order to execute this drill, simply make a shot and retrieve it, then hit another and retrieve it. In this way, you force yourself to move constantly and to hit with diversity. While the drill can be used to improve your total game, most players confine their choice of shotmaking to drops, corners, and reverse corners in the mid- and front court. Be careful in this drill of rapid movement and diverse shotmaking to avoid the tendency toward sloppy execution; make each shot crisply but properly.

Let us turn now from our analysis of each of the individual components of the game, to the specific problem of defeating an opponent.

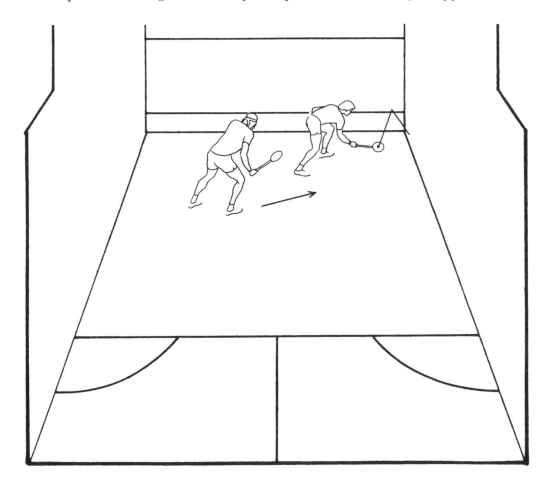

TACTICS AND STRATEGY

The various shots comprising the game of squash are the tools by which a player attempts to defeat his opponent. So far we have primarily discussed how one individual in a set position and with much time can execute these shots most effectively. However, this information is insufficient, for singles squash is played not by one but by two people forcing one another to hit on the run and from a position in the court far from the T. Under these less than ideal circumstances, the player who eventually will win the squash battle is the one who not only hits his shots most effectively but who also chooses the shot which will force his opponent to run the greatest distance in the least amount of time. The systematic selection of a particular *shot* is called tactics, while the systematic selection of a *series* of shots during a point, or of certain *types* of shots in a match, is called strategy. Together, tactics and strategy form the plan by which the player tries to increase his level of shotmaking and mobility *relative* to his opponent and thereby gain the decisive advantage which will win him the match.

TACTICS

Tactics in squash can best be defined as the reasoned employment of *a particular shot at a particular time* in order to gain the offensive advantage over one's opponent. While in the shotmaking and mobility sections we discussed *how* to make a shot properly, in the tactics section we shall discuss *when* to make a particular shot. In a game of such rapid movement and split-second timing as squash, a player simply does not have the time to analyze his present situation completely in order to ascertain the perfect shot for that situation. Consequently, certain methods for quickly determining the proper shot to use in a given situation are very important in squash. One method is to have certain rules of thumb, or automatics, at one's immediate disposal, which apply to *any* situation in which the player might find himself, and which reduce the time required for correct determination of the most effective shot.

AUTOMATICS

Automatic #1: Choose the shot that you are best able to hit and that your opponent is least able to return.

Many players commit the tactical error of assuming that simply because a particular shot works well against most opponents in most matches it will work well against every opponent in every match. Such an assumption is simply not true. It is quite possible that what is normally a player's best shot will not be accurate at all in a particular match, or will be that shot which the particular opponent returns best. Thus the key to hitting the proper shot in any situation on the court is for the player to be flexible; he must always choose that shot which he is most capable of making and which his opponent is least capable of returning.

Flexibility does not end once the player has initially determined his strong and weak shots relative to his opponent. During the course of any match, both the player's ability to hit a shot and his opponent's ability to return it can change radically. Therefore, an important corollary to this first automatic is that the player always be flexible enough to change his choice of shot when he finds that circumstances have changed.

Automatic #2: Always play the percentage shot.

The percentage shot is the one which is least likely to result in an error (i.e., hitting the tin) *and* that is most likely to put the opponent in a disadvantageous hitting position. In part, these percentage shots must be determined by the individual player based on his knowledge of his past ability and his present analysis of both his own and his opponent's shotmaking ability in that match. However, some general rules of thumb useful against any opponent also apply:

1. Never go for a winner while off balance or when hitting from the back court; always aim well above the tin to allow yourself time to return to the T and to force your opponent to move to the back court.

2. When your opponent is out of position and has made a shot for which you are well prepared and in good position, always go for a winner. Letting a good opportunity pass can be just as fatal as hitting the tin.

3. Immediately attack any ball which bounces in or passes through the midcourt area between the two service boxes; if a player can hit the ball in that part of the court the opponent must be off the T and susceptible to a putaway shot.

4. Wait until the last instant before starting any part of your foreswing when hitting a shot in the forecourt or back court; if a player is not on the T when hitting his shot he must assume that his opponent is. Thus, hesitation allows him the deception he crucially needs to make both a safe and effective shot.

To summarize these two rules: Pause in the back court or forecourt; attack immediately in midcourt.

Automatic #3: Vary your shots.

A player should attempt to use as many different, though still appropriate, shots in a given situation as possible, provided he can hit each one relatively well and provided that no one of the shots is being returned with too much accuracy by the opponent. Variation is important because it adds the vital element of surprise to the player's game. When the opponent is uncertain as to the particular shot he must retrieve, he is far less mobile and is therefore much less capable of hitting an effective return.

The previous automatics are extremely helpful for enabling the player to determine rapidly the best shot to employ at a particular time. However, because they give only a general tactical guideline, it is necessary to view the more specific situations in which the player might find himself. There are really only six tactical situations a player must master; these merely recur over and over in any match with only slight variations. The following discussion of each of these tactical situations includes the most effective shots and the optimal position in the court from which to achieve the highest degree of shotmaking effectiveness and mobility, while at the same time decreasing the degree of those elements for one's opponent. The shots are ordered according to the ease of hitting in the particular situation and the probable percentage of success the average player can expect to achieve. This ranking should be viewed and used very flexibly in order that the choice of shot be always based both on the individual's ability to hit the shot and upon his opponent's inability to return it in that match. Thus the reader may find that a shot which is here ranked fourth may be the shot that he hits best and/or that his opponent has the greatest difficulty returning. In such a case, the player should by all means use that shot most often, though still seeking diversity in his shots for the sake of surprise and deception.

SERVING SITUATION

This situation is the beginning of every point:

As server readies himself, receiver stands near vertical T line facing side wall with his racket back.

Server's Purpose. The server must drive the receiver deep and away from the T, forcing him either to hit the tin or to make a weak response which can easily be put away.

Server's Choice of Shots.

1. Lob: As the most effective and safest of any serve, the lob should be used most often in this situation.

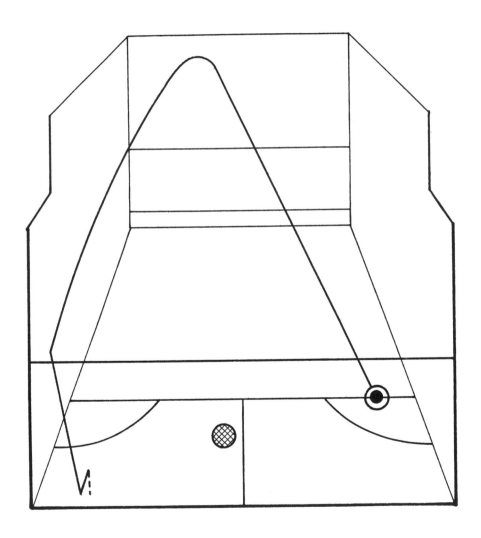

2. Hard or Slice: Normally these serves should be used only for variation and surprise. However, they may be used as the basic serve if the receiver is baffled by them or if the ceiling of the court is very low.

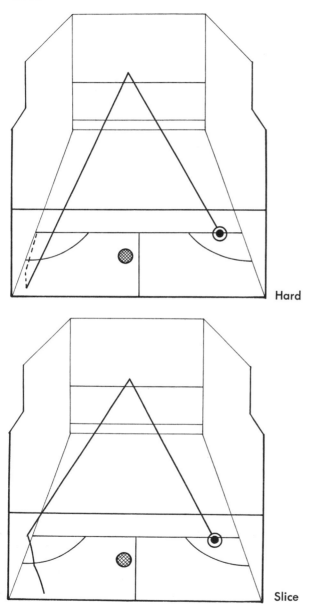

Hard

Slice

Receiver's Purpose. Usually, the receiver should hit deep to bring the server out of the center of the court so that he (the receiver) can take the T. The receiver may attempt a winner, but only if the serve is weak.

Receiver's Choice of Returns.

1. Deep Alley: The deep alley should be used most often because it best accomplishes the receiver's main purpose of forcing the server off the T. Moreover, it is difficult to return, since the server must contend with the side wall. The deep alley should bounce on the floor service line and stay close to the side wall.

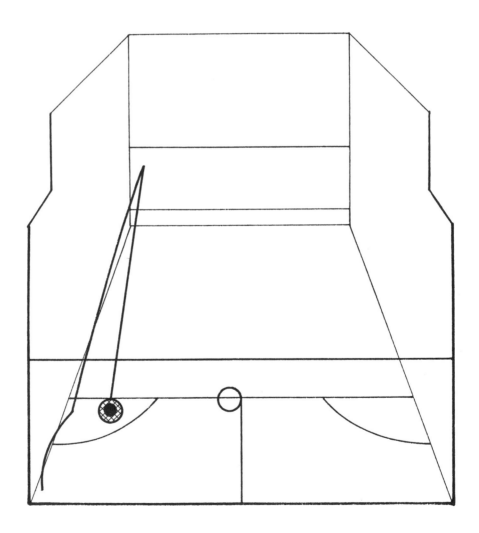

2. Fast Cross-Court: This return should usually be made as a variation from the deep alley. It should be hit as the server begins to inch closer to the side wall in expectation of the deep alley. The cross-court should be hit fast and aimed about 3 feet above the telltale line.

3. Drop: This shot is difficult to execute and should be used only when the receiver is very sure of his ability to hit the shot well. Even then, it should be employed only as an occasional changeup from the deep alley.

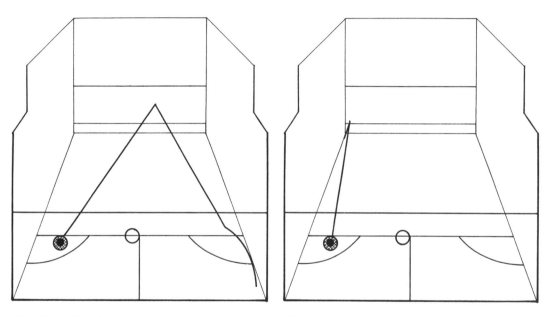

Fast Cross-Court   **Drop**

Server's Position on the T After Serving. The server should stand one step to the side of the T on which the receiver is returning the serve. This is because the deep alley is the most difficult to return of the receiver's possible responses and is also the most likely. But while the server should favor that side of the T, he should not do so by too much or the receiver will beat him with the cross-court.

While receiver hits ball above his head and far in front of his body, server stands one step to receiver's side of the T.

BACK COURT-ALONG-SIDE-WALL SITUATION

Probably the majority of shots in a good match are hit from this area of the court. The situation occurs when one player hits a deep passing shot, forcing the other player to move to the back court to return the shot.

Hitter, deep in back court, must force retriever, standing on the T, out of center court.

Hitter's Purpose. The hitter's purpose should almost always be to hit deep to move the opponent off the T. Attempting to make an immediate winner from deep in the back court usually results either in the ball's striking the tin or in the opponent's putting the ball away from his position on the T.

Hitter's Choice of Shots.

1. Deep Alley: The deep alley should normally be hit most often, both because it travels to and from the front wall faster than any other deep shot and because it forces the opponent to contend with the side wall.

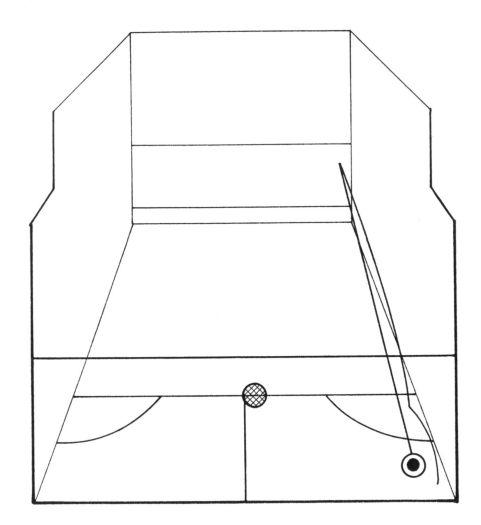

2. Deep Cross-Court: The deep cross-court should be used primarily as a variation from the deep alley, as the cross-court is usually the easier of the two shots for the T player to intercept for a winner. The deep cross-court works best when the player on the T inches too close to the side wall, expecting a deep alley. It should be hit fast and two feet above the tell-tale so that it breaks low off the side wall at about the floor service line.

3. Alley and Cross-Court Lobs: If the opponent on the T is a very good volleyer or if the court is slow (the ball does not rebound off the front wall as fast in some courts as in others), these lobs should be used in place of the deep alley and deep cross-court. The lob should be aimed high on the front wall and can be hit with underspin or topspin. In either case, it should be hit with a firm wrist.

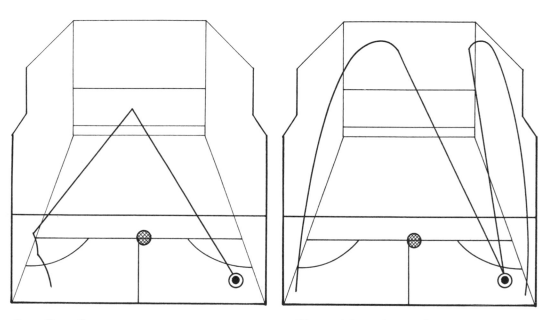

Deep Cross-Court   Alley and Cross-Court Lobs

4. 3-Wall Shot: Again, this shot is used as a deceptive variation from the deep alley. The 3-wall shot can be hit simply as a means to force the opponent to the front court or it can be hit for a winner when the opponent becomes used to moving to the back court to retrieve the deep alley.

5. Roll Corner: This shot too can be used when the opponent gets into the habit of moving to the back court to retrieve the deep alley. However, it should be used sparingly or it becomes an easy shot for the opponent to put away.

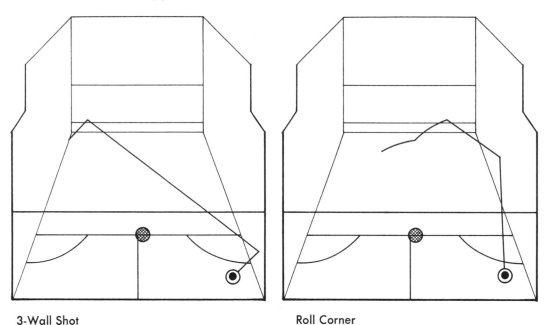

3-Wall Shot   Roll Corner

Purpose of Player on the T. The player on the T holds the vital center court, so his task is to maintain control of this area and to win the point.

Choice of Returns for Player on the T. The player's choice of returns depends upon the particular shot hit by the player in the back court and upon the degree of effectiveness with which that shot is hit. If the back-court player has used a deep passing shot and has executed it well, the player on the T must move to the back court to make his return. In this case, his choice of shots is exactly the same as for the player who has just hit. If the player in the back court has hit a deep shot which is inaccurate, the player on the T should go for a winner. His choices in this case are outlined later in Situation #4. Proper responses to the 3-wall shot and the roll corner are discussed in Situations #5 and #6.

Position of the Player on the T. Since the deep alley is the most difficult and thus the most likely shot the player on the T must return, he should stand one step to the side of the T where the player in the back court is hitting. But again, he must not move too far in this direction or the player in the back court will hit a cross-court for a winner.

With retriever now deep in back court, former hitter takes ready position one step to the right of the T.

BACK COURT-IN-CENTER SITUATION

This situation usually occurs when a lob serve is hit so hard that it bounces first on the back wall and then on the floor and comes out into the middle. It also results when a cross-court strikes the side wall too high so that the ball does not die in back as it should. Finally, the situation arises when the player on the T chooses not to volley a ball which passes through midcourt because the shot is over his head or is moving too fast.

Having backed retriever close to one side wall, hitter executes deep putaway.

Hitter's Purpose. The hitter should attempt to put away any ball that comes out a reasonable distance from the back wall.

Hitter's Choice of Shots.

1. Low and Fast Alley Shot: On the average, the low and fast alley shot should be used most often when this situation arises. This is because the retriever is backed up against one side wall so that the entire other side of the court is open. Thus the retriever must run almost the width of the court to get the shot, if it is hit reasonably well. The player must not rush his shot or the retriever will be able to begin movement sooner to return it. Moreover, the player must be careful not to aim too close to the tin, since the hitting situation is one in which the player must back up quickly to execute his shot.

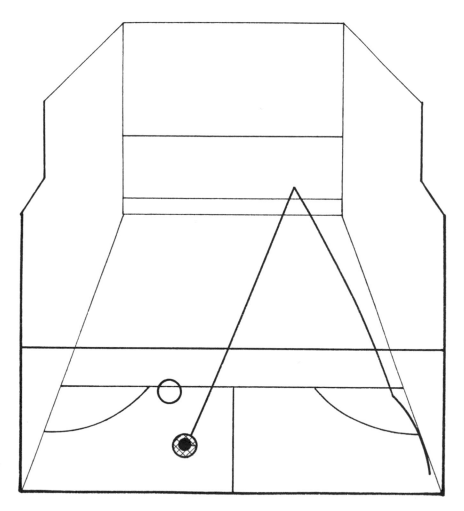

2. Low and Fast Cross-Court: This shot is used when the hitter sees the retriever trying to start early to get the low alley, the shot usually hit in this situation. The low cross-court is hit off the same stroke as the alley so that, ideally, the retriever is caught going the wrong way (countermotion). The shot should be used only sparingly, however, or the surprise, and thus the effectiveness, of the shot is lost.

In making both of these shots, the player should hesitate until the instant when the ball has come all the way down to knee level before starting the foreswing. As mentioned previously, this hesitation gives the player much more power and deception in his shot.

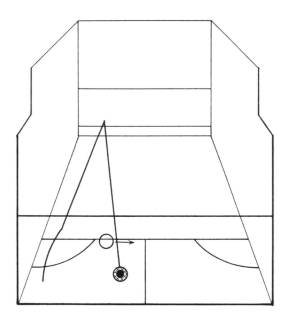

Retriever's Purpose. The retriever is out of position and in grave danger of losing the point. His only purpose is somehow to retrieve the hitter's attempted winner, hopefully in such a way that he will have time to get back into good position on the T. Under no circumstance should the retriever go for a winner himself.

Retriever's Choice of Shots. Defensive Alley Lob (Defensive Deep Game): The alley lob should be hit every time in this situation, because it is the only shot which will achieve the retriever's two-part purpose of preventing immediate loss of the point and of gaining enough time to get back to good position on the T before the opponent hits again.

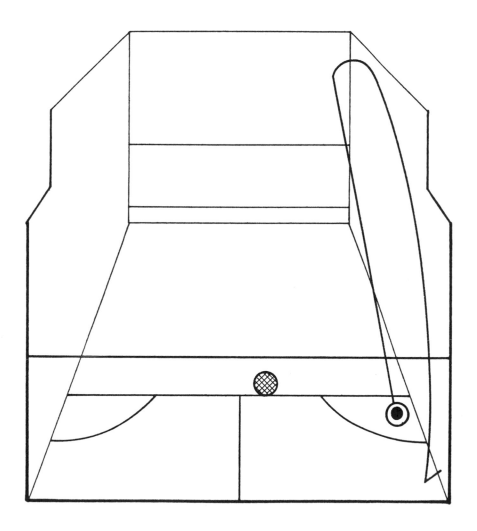

Retriever's Court Position. The retriever should attempt to get as close to the T as possible without having to draw back at the last moment to avoid being hit by the opponent's racket.

Retriever faces opposite side wall, wrist cocked, and prepares to move to ball.

MIDCOURT SITUATION

Usually, this situation results when a player in the *back court along the side wall* makes a mistake while trying to move his opponent off the T. His shot may nick the side wall going up or back, thus coming to the middle, it may not go deep enough, or it may not travel close enough to the side wall during its flight. All of these errors enable the player to hit from midcourt.

With retriever in back court, hitter executes putaway from midcourt.

Hitter's Purpose. The player should almost always go for a winner.

Hitter's Choice of Shots. The player can hit more shots from midcourt than from any other place in the court. In most of the other situations, the player has one shot which is preferable to the others. In the midcourt situation, however, the wise player is the one who constantly varies his shots. The main determinants of the choice of shot are (1) the hitter's ability to hit a particular shot well, (2) his opponent's ability to return the shot effectively, and (3) the relative position of hitter to retriever.

This situation is divided into four subsituations, based on the hitter's position relative to both the T and to the retriever. The subsituations and the best shots to be employed in each depend upon whether the hitter is closer to the T or closer to the side wall and upon whether the hitter and the retriever are on the same or on different sides of the court. Because of the importance of diverse shotmaking in the midcourt situation, the shots proposed for each subsituation are not necessarily listed in order of effectiveness.

HITTER IN CENTER, HITTER AND RETRIEVER ON SAME SIDE OF COURT

1. Corner: The corner is effective in this situation because it ends in the extreme opposite spot in the court to where the retriever is positioned.

2. Alley: This shot is *only* effective when the player has executed a few soft corner shots in the same situation. The fast alley is made with a ground stroke intially similar to that used for the corner but ends in the opposite extreme of the court. However, unless the opponent is deceived into thinking that a corner shot is to be used, he will be in perfect position to make a return.

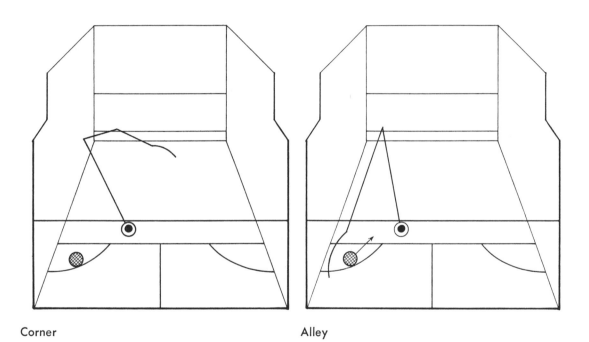

Corner   Alley

3. Drop: The drop is probably a deadlier shot in this situation than the corner, since the drop forces the retriever to contend with the side wall. But again, the player is wise to use both shots until circumstances dictate that one is far more effective than the other.

4. Reverse Drop: Like the corner, the reverse drop ends in the extreme opposite part of the court from the retriever. In addition, the reverse drop dies near the side wall. As a result, it is probably the most effective of any shot in this situation. However, the reverse drop is a difficult shot to execute well and should be tried only if the player has fine touch and has practiced the shot considerably.

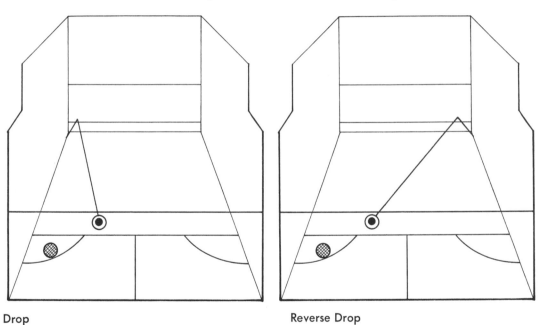

Drop   Reverse Drop

5. Cross-Court: This shot is very effective if the player attacks the ball and hits with underspin so that the ball dies quickly.

6. Quick-Snap Cross-Court: This apparent short shot should be used whenever the retriever, in expectation of the short putaway, has begun to run hard toward the front wall.

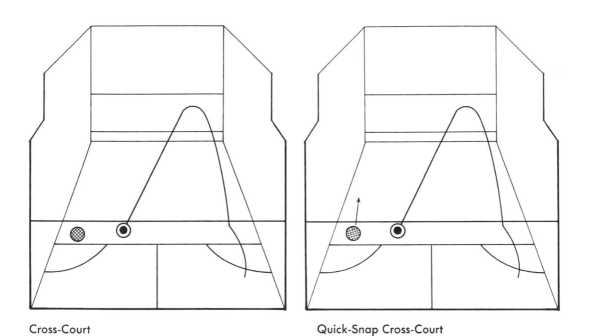

Cross-Court   Quick-Snap Cross-Court

HITTER IN CENTER, HITTER AND RETRIEVER ON OPPOSITE SIDES OF COURT

1. Drop: In this situation, the drop is the most deadly shot because it places the ball in the extreme opposite part of the court from the retriever and dies near the side wall.

2. Low, Fast Alley: The low, fast alley is also effective in this case and does not have to be hit with as much control and accuracy as the drop shot.

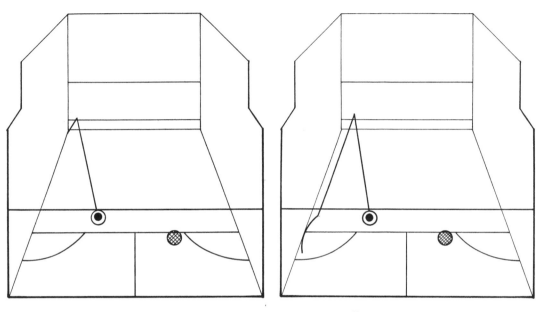

Drop   Low, Fast Alley

3. Reverse Corner: This difficult shot, while very effective, should only be used if the player is highly adept at executing it.

4. Quick-Snap Alley: This shot is used when the hitter suspects that the retriever is rapidly moving to the front wall to get the possible short shot.

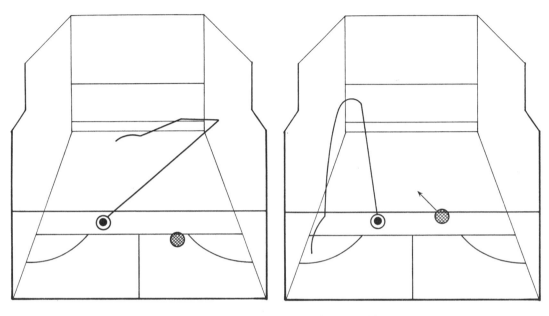

Reverse Corner   Quick-Snap Alley

HITTER NEAR SIDE WALL, HITTER AND RETRIEVER ON SAME SIDE OF COURT

When a player must execute a shot close to the side wall he has less time to get set and has a smaller variety of potential shots than usual. Under these conditions, a general rule applies: The safest and most effective shots the player can use when he must hit close to the side wall are usually those hit fast, deep, and down the line (along that side wall). The player who follows this rule will avoid using shots such as the corner or reverse corner, which are either ineffective or nonpercentage in this particular situation. In adhering to this rule, however, the player must be certain not to neglect variety in his shot-making or he will become predictable.

1. Fast Alley: This shot should be hit low and fast unless the hitter thinks his opponent has had time to reach the T. In that case, he should aim about 3 feet above the tin to send the ball deep.

2. Drop: The drop is effective here but should be used only if the hitter has time and is set.

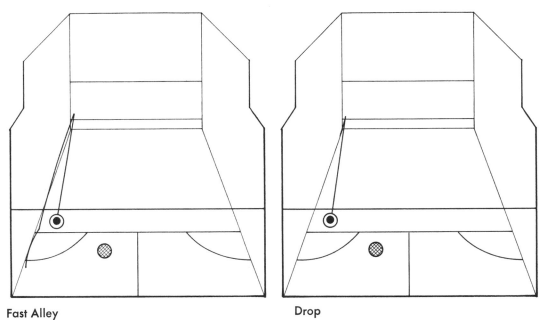

Fast Alley   Drop

3. Reverse Drop: The reverse drop is difficult to hit when the player is close to the side wall. Moreover, the shot loses some of its effectiveness when it is hit close to the side wall because, in this situation, the retriever is near the T and is moving rapidly forward as the shot is being executed. Thus, while it can be a good shot, the reverse drop should be used sparingly here and only when the player has excellent touch.

4. Quick-Snap Alley: Again, this shot is employed when the hitter feels his opponent moving forward rapidly in expectation of a touch shot.

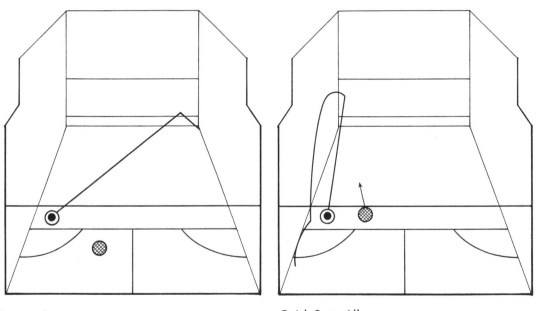

Reverse Drop   Quick-Snap Alley

HITTER NEAR SIDE WALL, HITTER AND RETRIEVER ON OPPOSITE SIDES OF COURT

Again, because the hitter must move farther from the T to make his shot, he should emphasize shots which are very fast and which require the least amount of pinpoint accuracy.

1. Alley: The alley is again the hitter's best choice when he is close to the side wall. As before, the alley should be hit low and fast unless the hitter feels his opponent has had time to reach the T. In that case, the shot should be sent deep.

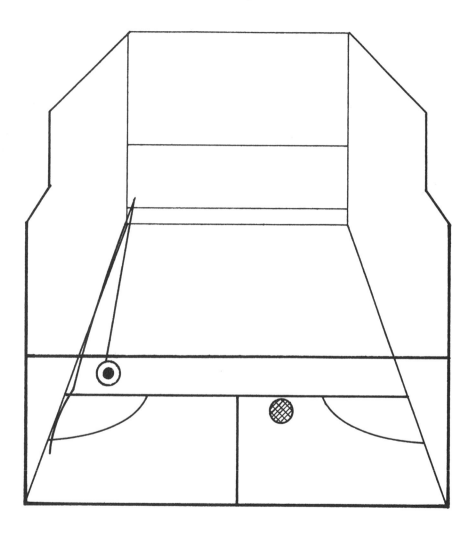

2. Drop
3. Quick-Snap Alley

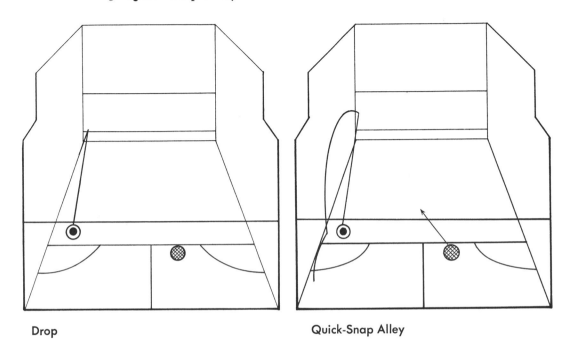

Drop   Quick-Snap Alley

Retriever's Purpose. The retriever is usually moving toward the T when the hitter makes his shot but he is still out of position. His only purpose is to get his opponent's attempted winner and to make a shot which will allow him to get back into position on the T.

Retriever's Choice of Shots. The retriever's choice of shots again depends upon which shot the hitter has used and how effectively it has been hit. Usually, the retriever must move very fast to the front wall to get the hitter's shot (see Situation #5).

Retriever's Court Position. As in Situation #3, the retriever is out of position in the back court. Obviously, he must try to get to the T position as soon as possible. However, he must also be certain to stop his forward movement and quickly assume the ready position as soon as he sees that the hitter is about to execute his shot. In this way, the retriever is not caught in countermotion and has the best chance of returning the greatest number of shots.

As hitter begins his foreswing, retriever takes ready position, no matter how far he is from the T.

FRONT-COURT SITUATION (A)

This situation occurs when one player, having the offensive advantage, has gone for a winner and the other player, on the defensive, is running very fast to the front court to get the shot. It is the situation which immediately follows the midcourt situation, the retriever in that situation having now become the hitter and vice versa.

Hitter's Purpose. The hitter is running desperately just to get to the ball before it dies and thus he must first prevent outright loss of the point. As a secondary purpose, he wants to hit a shot which will enable him to take over the T.

Hitter's Choice of Shots. Since the hitter is running at top speed to get his opponent's shot, he will be facing the front wall when he reaches the ball. For this reason, most players hit a hard and low cross-court, as the natural, and thus the easiest, swing in this difficult situation is across the front of the body. Unfortunately, the easiest shot for the hitter to execute is also the easiest for the retriever to put away.

Hitter makes desperate lunge for ball while retriever assumes that ball will be returned.

Instead of the cross-court, the hitter should employ one of the shots of the defensive short game. In these shots, the spear stroke is used, power being furnished not by a big swing but rather by a flick of the wrist. With this stroke the hitter can send the ball both short and deep and do so with more control and deception.

1. Spear Drop: The best shot by far in this situation is the spear drop. This shot is difficult for the player on the T to return for a winner because he must contend with the side wall. Also, since the spear drop comes out only a short distance from the front wall, it can win the point outright if the player on the T is not alert. Finally, the spear drop allows the hitter to get into a better position, because the player on the T must move a considerable distance to retrieve the short drop.

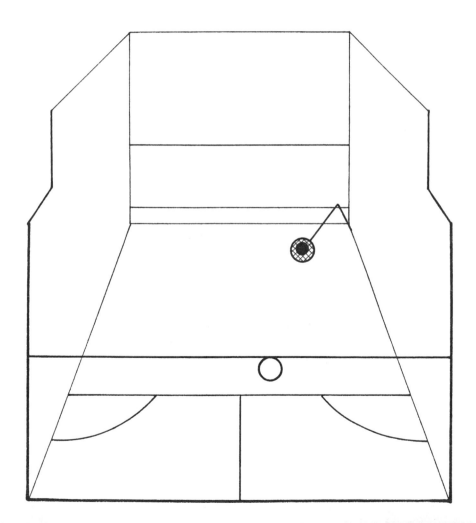

2. Spear Cross-Court: The player on the T, upon seeing the hitter about to employ the spear stroke, will often move close behind the hitter in expectation of the drop. If the hitter senses this forward movement, he is wise to use the spear cross-court, which is the deep variation of the spear drop. The shot is risky, however, if the player originally on the T has *not* moved up close to the front wall to return the spear drop.

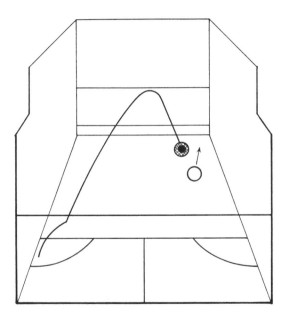

Retriever's Purpose. The retriever in this case is well-positioned on the T and may not have to return his opponent's shot at all if his attempted winner is good enough. However, the retriever *must assume that the hitter will reach the ball in time.* As Coach Edwin Reade of Deerfield Academy states, the player should figure on winning the point on the shot he hits *after* he has made the short shot.[5] The retriever's purpose, then, is to be ready to make another putaway shot, which the opponent, now in poor position up front, cannot return.

Retriever's Choice of Shots. To best accomplish his purpose, the retriever must attack the ball. The hitter, far from the T, is trying to return there quickly. Consequently, the sooner the retriever makes his shot, the farther away from the T is the former hitter.

1. Low, Fast Alley (Offensive Deep Game): The low, fast alley shot which dies in the back court is usually the most effective shot in this situation especially when the former hitter is still close to the front wall. Even when the former hitter is nearer the T, the alley is a good shot because the hitter is moving backward quickly and cannot make the sideward movement which retrieval of the alley requires. The alley is especially good if the hitter has mistakenly tried a cross-court, since the alley ends in the extreme opposite corner of the court from the hitter.

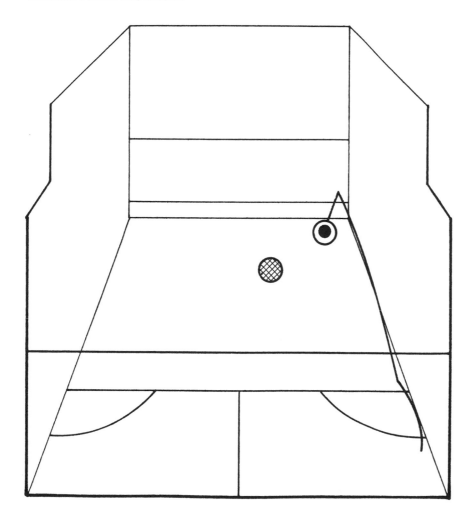

2. Drop: If the former hitter is close to the T but has not arrived there yet, this deceptive variation of the alley shot can be most effective. The hitter is backpedaling quickly, trying to be ready for the fast alley shot. The drop shot catches him going in exactly the wrong direction (countermotion). If the hitter is still close to the front wall when the retriever begins his shot, however, the drop should not be used.

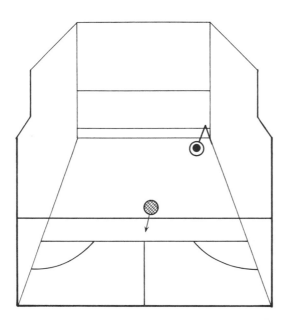

Retriever's Position on the T. The retriever should take a position on the T which will enable him to get the most difficult shots the hitter can make without leaving himself open to those shots which are normally less effective. In order of difficulty, the shots the retriever must face are the spear drop, the spear cross-court, and the hard and low cross-court. With this in mind, the retriever should stand 1 step in front of the T and 1 step to the side of the T on which the hitter is making his shot. The retriever must not move too far forward or too close to the side wall in expectation of the spear drop, or he may find himself vulnerable to the cross-court shot.

As hitter moves to ball, retriever takes ready position forward and to one side of the T.

FRONT-COURT SITUATION (B)

In this situation the hitter is in the front court and has sufficient time to hit his shot with the standard swing. Front-court situation (B) usually occurs when the hitter in the midcourt situation has made an ineffective putaway shot so that use of the spear stroke is not required. The situation also arises when the opponent hits a defensive alley lob which strikes the side wall.

With more time, hitter executes putaway while retriever waits alertly.

Hitter's Purpose. Though the retriever is the one who is standing on the T in this situation, the hitter has the offensive advantage and should usually go for the winner.

Hitter's Choice of Shots. No one shot in this situation is vastly better than any other. The best results are achieved when a variety of shots are employed, as this keeps the retriever guessing. No matter which shot the hitter uses, he *must wait* as long as possible before making it so that deception will be high. Rushing the shot is always disastrous here, because it enables the retriever, already positioned on the T, to anticipate the putaway attempt and to hit deep for a winner.

The hitter must also be certain to accomplish all preswing movements—facing the side wall, getting the racket back, proper judgment-footwork—since this increases the power, control, and deception he can achieve when making his shot.

1. Cross-Court: The low and fast cross-court shot which hits the side wall just above the floor service line is potentially the most powerful and deceptive of the many shots the hitter can use. It is an especially effective shot when the retriever moves up close behind the hitter in expectation of a short shot.

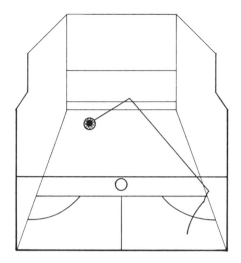

Cross-Court

2. Drop: The drop shot is a good variation from the cross-court because it ends in the opposite extreme from the cross-court. However, the player must be certain to hit the drop with a stroke similar to that used for the cross-court or his opponent will have an easy putaway.

3. Alley: A final shot which should be used alternately with the cross-court and the drop is the alley shot. Though it is not as potentially powerful or deceptive as the cross-court, the alley has the important advantage of hugging the side wall during its flight, making it difficult to return.

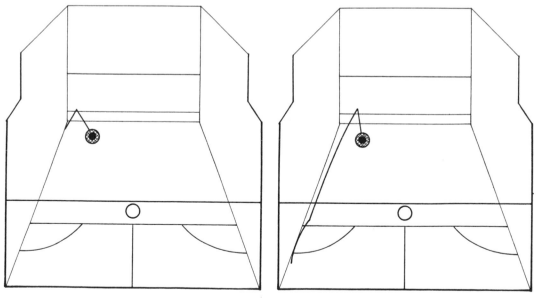

Drop   Alley

Retriever's Purpose. Realizing that the hitter will go for a winner, the retriever first must prevent outright loss of the point. Second, the retriever must be alert, ready to attack the ball and go for a winner himself, if the hitter makes a poor shot.

Retriever's Choice of Shots. The deep alley shot is by far the best choice for the retriever in this situation. If the hitter's shot is good, a deep alley gives the retriever time to move to the T. If the hitter's shot is poor, the deep alley enables the retriever to win the point outright, since the former hitter is far out of position in the front court.

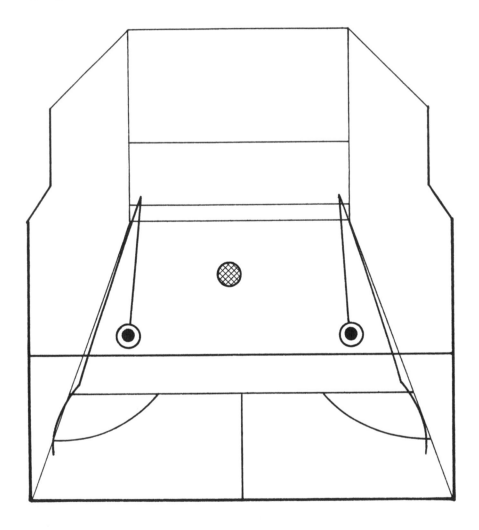

Retriever's Position on the T. At first, the retriever must assume that the hitter will employ the cross-court, the drop, and the alley equally often. Consequently, at the beginning, he should play about 1 step in front of the T, because this spot allows the retriever to get to each of the three shots equally well. However, if the retriever sees that the hitter favors one shot above the other two, he should adjust his position slightly to enable himself to get to that shot more easily. Again, the retriever should not adjust too far in any one direction or he will be unprepared for either of the other two shots his opponent might use.

Retriever waits for hitter's shot one step in front of the T.

TACTICAL PRACTICE

Tactical practice consists basically of two activities. The first is repetition of a single shot from the particular spot on the court from which the shot is most usually executed in a game situation. This ensures that the player's stroke will be second nature to him, thus saving valuable time during an actual point, and preventing costly error. The second major activity in tactical practice involves the use and variation of all the different shots possible in one tactical situation. This activity trains the player to recognize immediately a great number of shot possibilities, and to remember which shot he himself last used in the same situation. This ability is critical in the rapid pace of the actual match situation. Of the six tactical situations, not all require that the player employ both types of drill to the same degree. A short summary of the best sort of practice to use for each tactical situation follows.

1. Serving Situation: Serving and returning serve do not require split-second thinking; they demand a highly-controlled and very consistent shot. To develop control and consistency when practicing the serve, hit a series of one kind of serve from one of the two serving quarter-circles. Then repeat the same series from the other quarter-circle. Do this for each kind of serve. Concentrate on the all-important lob. When working on the return of serve, have a partner hit you a series of one kind of serve and make a proper return. Emphasize the alley shot. Execute a series of returns on the other side of the court, and then repeat the entire process for the other two kinds of serve.

2. Back Court-Along-Side-Wall Situation: Again this tactical situation involves relatively little shot choice and seldom requires quick decision-making. Emphasis should therefore be placed on the repetition of one shot, followed by the repetition of the other shot possibilities. The best method of gaining this particular kind of practice is to simulate a deep-game battle for the T with another player: Stand in one of the back corners with the ball in your left hand, and have a partner stand on the T. Hit a deep passing shot down the rail and switch places with your partner on the T. Continue this process until a high degree of proficiency in hitting the deep alley is achieved.

The player standing on the T should be careful not to cut the ball off and volley for a winner unless his partner's shot from the back court is especially poor, since this destroys the repetition, and thus the effectiveness, of the drill. Again, once one shot has been practiced sufficiently, the players should proceed to the other shot possibilities in the situation.

3. Back-Wall-in-Middle Situation: In this tactical situation, the hitter may use one of two shots, of which the alley is much preferred. The retriever may properly employ only one shot, the defensive alley lob. To practice the offensive shots comprising this situation, stand inside the vertical T line and have your partner stand near the opposite service quarter-circle. Have him hit cross-courts which travel higher and deeper than a properly executed cross-court, thus allowing you to take the shot off the back wall. Execute the correct alley shot (backing up quickly with hips low and knees bent) and then repeat the entire process. In the course of this exercise, hit the cross-court occasionally in order to establish that shot in your mind as an important alternative.

To practice the defensive alley lob in a simulated game situation, crouch near one side wall and have your partner execute the offensive alley shot from the appropriate court position. At the right moment, slide quickly across the court and make the alley lob. Repeat this process until you have gained a reasonable proficiency, and then practice the same shot from the other side of the court.

4. Midcourt Situation: This situation, or more exactly, the many subsituations comprising the midcourt game, is one in which success is determined largely by the variety of shots the player employs. The situation is also characterized by the need for rapid decision-making. Consequently, most of the tactical practice done by the player should consist of standing in one area of the midcourt and alternately hitting each of the shots appropriate to that court position. The player may execute this drill alone, or, for greater efficiency, have a partner hit the ball to him and then quickly retrieve each shot. It must be emphasized, however, that drills in which the player executes one shot over and over are important, too, and should also be used.

5. Front-Court Situation A: Like the first three tactical situations, the front-court situation A involves few shot possibilities, and
one of these, the "flip" drop shot, is highly preferable. Once again,
the player should practice primarily by executing one shot, usually
the flip drop, over and over until it becomes second nature.

To execute this drill, stand to one side of the T and take the
ready position. Hit, or have a partner hit, a drop shot to that corner
of the front and side walls nearest you. As soon as the ball is struck,
move quickly but smoothly to the front wall and execute the flip
drop shot. Repeat the process a number of times, but occasionally
employ the proper variation to the flip drop, the flip cross-court, in
order to gain practice at changing your choice of shot while running
at top speed. Repeat the process from the other side of the T.

6. Front-Court Situation B: Because this tactical situation is one
in which the offensive player has only three shots, each of approximately equal utility, tactical practice should consist primarily of
hitting a succession of the different possible shots one after the other.
However, because the hitter in this situation is far out of center court
while the retriever is well-positioned on the T, accuracy in shotmaking is critical just to avoid outright loss of the point. Thus, in practice, the player should also use repetition drills to best refine each
shot.

To practice the shots in this tactical situation, stand a few feet
in front of the T and a little to one side. Then toss the ball to the
front wall so that its rebound provides you with enough time to move
forward and set up for the putaway shot. Correctly execute one of
the shots appropriate to this situation. Repeat this process a number
of times, but use a different shot each time. Do the same drill a little
to the other side of the T with the opposite ground stroke.

STRATEGY

Strategy in squash is defined as the reasoned employment of *a combination of shots during a point and of certain types of shots during a match* so as to gain the decisive advantage over one's opponent. In both tactics and strategy, the player attempts to force his opponent to hit from a weak position, thereby decreasing his level of mobility and shotmaking ability. The *difference* between tactics and strategy is in the scale and the method by which this purpose is achieved. In tactics, the player attempts to force his opponent to hit from a weak position *on a particular shot.* He does this by making his opponent run the greatest distance and/or by causing him to use his worst shot. In strategy, the player attempts to force his opponent to hit from a weak position *during a series of shots* in a point and *throughout the entire match.* Here the decisive advantage is gained by attacking the entire areas of the opponent's shotmaking ability and mobility which are his weakest.

The strategic attack should take three forms: type, placement, and tempo of the shot the player uses. For example, when playing against an opponent who has difficulty returning the alley shot, the player should hit the alley most of the time. When playing against an opponent who cannot hit effective shots in the front court, the player should use his short game whenever feasible. When playing against an opponent who needs a lot of time to execute his shots, the player should use the volley as much as possible. Each of these basic methods enables the player to attack the weakest areas of an opponent's game. As in the case of tactics, the key to strategy is to determine the opponent's weakness as accurately and as quickly as possible. The following are a few important automatics which will force any opponent to hit from a weak position at all times.

Automatic #1: Choose the series and the type of shot that you are best able to hit and that your opponent is least able to return.

This rule of thumb, almost identical to that in the tactics section, serves to reemphasize the importance of taking the opponent into account in determining a strategy. Two examples readily illustrate this principle. A player who normally gives only limited use to the volley in his game may find that this is virtually the only type of shot which works successfully against his particular opponent. Conversely, a player who normally gains most of his success from hitting hard may find that his opponent is extremely adept at defeating such a power game. In both cases, the player would be wise to change from his usual style of play as soon as possible and to determine and execute the strategy which will allow him the best chance of defeating his opponent. So in order to win, the player must determine his strengths and weaknesses relative to those of his opponent and must execute those strengths as soon as possible. But again, a strategy ploy which is initially successful may not be enough; the relative strengths and weaknesses of each player often change drastically during the course of a match, especially if the particular strategy the player is using involves only a limited number of different types of shots. If the player is to retain the fullest advantage over his opponent throughout the match, he must remain flexible and be prepared to adjust when any change in relative strengths and weaknesses demands it.

Automatic #2: Play the percentages.

Related to strategy, percentage play is the reasoned employment of a specific series of shots in a point and of specific types of shots during the match which will most likely give the player the *advantage* and allow him to win the most points *over the long run* of the match. Coach Barnaby has analyzed strategic percentage play in terms of four levels of ability: beginner, intermediate, advanced, and expert. Using the basic characteristics that players of the same general level of play tend to exhibit as a guide, Barnaby has outlined the specific determinants of strategic percentage play for individuals in each of those levels.

BEGINNER

Characteristics:
1. Has practically no shots
   Strategic Percentage Play:
2. Aim well above the tin at all times so as to keep the ball in play.

INTERMEDIATE

Characteristics:
1. Has one pet shot he likes to make but lacks an assortment of shots.
   Strategic Percentage Play:
1. Figure out which side of your opponent's game is weakest and then pound that spot incessantly until an error gives you the point or an inaccuracy gives you a chance to play your pet shot.
2. Aim well above the tin at all times except when the ball is set up for your pet shot.

ADVANCED

Characteristics:
1. Has solid strokes on both sides
2. Can volley
3. Can deal reasonably decisively with any good opportunity on either side
   Strategic Percentage Play:
1. Fight for position (as opposed to fighting for the point). If you allow your opponent to attack, he is likely to win the point.
2. When a setup does occur, use a two-shot play: Drop or corner, then slam for depth.

A one-shot winner is nonpercentage because too many errors accompany the aces. It takes one shot—the short one—to get your opponent far enough out of position so that a winner is possible.

EXPERT

Characteristics:
1. Has excellent strokes
2. Has extreme mobility
3. Has all the shots

Strategic Percentage Play:
1. Never try for a winner; against an expert, the ball would have to hit below the top of the tin to be an outright winner.
2. Keep your opponent constantly on the move.
3. Try to fool him.[6]
4. Using Barnaby's system, let us add yet another strategic automatic, which can and should be used by the advanced and expert players to gain the advantage over their opponent: When hitting ground strokes in which the ball has not rebounded from the back wall, attack the ball while it is rising, and, if possible, just after it has bounced on the floor (even though this is not the "ideal hitting position").

It would not be an exaggeration to say that 90 percent of the game of squash at the upper levels of ability is played and won in the midcourt. Within this small strip, the quicker the player makes his shot, the farther his opponent will be from the T.

5. Given the importance at this level of play of countermotion, a corollary to the preceding automatic can be stated: Send most "quick-hit" ground strokes hard, low, and cross-court. The player, of course, must realize that these shots seldom produce outright winners, but their effect in disrupting the opponent's timing is often the single decisive factor in a match of top-flight play.

POINT STRATEGY

These strategic automatics provide the player with the *general* guidelines for gaining the advantage over his opponent. Such rules of thumb, while necessary, are not specific enough to enable the player to pinpoint the weaknesses of a particular opponent. Of course, matches are comprised of individual points, so a fuller and more specific presentation of strategy must begin with an analysis of the various ways of hitting a *series* of shots, in order to have the best chance of winning each point.

PATTERNS OF ATTACK

In simple terms, squash is a game in which the player attempts to force his opponent to cover too great a distance to make a return before the ball bounces a second time. Because of the spatial limitations of the squash court, the player cannot accomplish this end unless he first moves his opponent away from the optimal center-court area. Thus effective strategy during a point consists of hitting a *related series* of shots designed to move the opponent out of position and so place him at the greatest disadvantage. These related series of shots, when seen whole, constitute patterns of attack.

Given the various shots of the deep and short games, a player can use any number of combinations of shots, or patterns of attack, to force the opponent out of position. However, because the squash court is longer than it is wide, the most effective way to gain the offensive and finally the decisive advantage over the opponent is to move him lengthwise. Based on this logic of lengthwise movement, four patterns emerge as central to the game of squash, three of which are variations of one basic pattern. The basic pattern of attack is called "deep-short-deep," and consists of the player's first hitting to the back court, then executing a short shot when his opponent makes a weak return, and finally hitting to the back court again to finish the point. This pattern expresses an entire method of attack which is primary to the game of squash, because in it the player uses the tool of superior shotmaking to directly affect his opponent's movement, driving him progressively farther out of position until he is finally unable to make a return. The other three patterns are variations of the first pattern, and exhibit an indirect, or secondary, method of attack. In these variations, the player uses the basic pattern of attack to deceive his opponent into *moving himself* away from where the ball is to land.

THE "DEEP-SHORT-DEEP" PATTERN

As the primary method of attack, the deep-short-deep pattern is the one upon which all others are based. It is also the safest means of defeating the opponent, since the ball is hit always to a vacant extreme of the court. Thus the deep-short-deep should be used more often than any other pattern of attack, especially at the beginning of a game and match, and when the opponent begins to anticipate the player's deceptive variations in attack. On the other hand, the deceptive variations become much more important later in the game and match, and are virtually a necessity if a player is to win consistently against the best opponents:

1. Deep (Struggle for the T): The pattern begins with the player hitting deep to the back court in a struggle for the T. This continues until the player gains the offensive advantage, due either to his own good shot or his opponent's error.

Left. Player hits deep to move opponent off the T.

Right. Opponent attempts deep passing shot but mistakenly hits ball too low on front wall.

2. Short (Offensive Short Game): With his opponent out of position in the back court, the player hits short in an attempt to win the point outright, or at least to draw his opponent even farther out of position.

3. Deep (Offensive Deep Game): Assuming that the opponent retrieves the short shot, the player executes the decisive hard and deep putaway shot, whether the opponent has hit short or deep. This final shot gains its effectiveness from the fact that the ball is not only traveling fast and low to the floor, but is also moving away from the opponent *and* the front wall.

Left. Player executes short putaway.

Middle. As opponent backs up, player executes deep putaway along wall.

Right. Ball dies in back court with opponent far away.

To summarize, four ingredients comprise the successful basic pattern of attack:

1. Getting maximum power, control, and deception desired in the shot
2. Being patient when out of position in the back court; that is, using only deep passing shots until one of the opponent's passing shots is weak enough that it can be attacked
3. Attacking the ball and immediately going for the short winner when such a weak response does occur
4. Hitting deep to the back corner when the opponent returns the touch shot

DECEPTIVE VARIATIONS FROM THE BASIC PATTERN

At the beginning of any game and match, the opponent is never sure of a player's shot preferences. Therefore, that opponent must always hesitate before moving to make a return. In this situation, the basic pattern of attack, in which each shot is hit to that area farthest from the opponent's court position, is the best one. On the other hand, as game and match progress, the opponent begins to expect the basic pattern, and tends to move automatically to certain spots on the court to retrieve the player's shots. Consequently, any variation the player makes in the basic pattern will, if executed suddenly and deceptively, catch the opponent going the wrong way. Such variations represent a *short-circuiting* of the basic pattern, and together constitute the second method by which a player can attack his opponent. Each of the three variations to the basic pattern short-circuits the basic pattern at a different stage of its three-part development. The first, the "deep-fake deep," involves the use of the 3-wall shot or the roll corner when it appears that the opponent has become used to moving to the back court in the battle for the T. The second patterned variation, the "deep-fake short," involves the use of the various deep flip shots when the opponent suspects the short putaway shot. The third variation, the "deep-short-fake deep," involves the use of either a touch shot, a 3-wall, or a roll corner (depending on the player's hitting position) when the opponent scrambles hard to the back court after retrieving the player's short putaway.

These deceptive variations are, in every sense of the word, investments. The use of a deceptive variation always involves a risk, because the short-circuiting shot necessarily travels to a spot in the court on or near the area in which the opponent has just been standing. For this reason, many adequate and even good players shy away from using the deceptive variations in hopes of winning by playing safe. But in so doing, these players ensure that they will never improve because, as investments, these trick patterns are necessary tools for defeating the better players. If employed at the right time, the deceptive variation has the effect of adding five to ten feet to the distance the opponent must travel to reach the ball, due to the countermotion these variations induce. Such an added distance is crucial against the higher-level players who can reach every undisguised shot in the game. Of course, if the opponent never adjusts to the basic pattern, the player should continue its use. But against the more experienced opponents, adjustment is usually rapid and complete. The keynote, then, is to use these variations *at the right time*. If they are set up by strict use of the basic pattern at the beginning of each game (especially the first), and if they are executed properly, the deceptive variations can be devastating. If they are employed too soon in the match or too often, they become self-defeating.

THE "DEEP-FAKE DEEP" PATTERN

Because so much of squash consists of a battle for the T, an opponent often will automatically start to move to the back court when he sees the player begin to execute a shot from one of the back corners of the court. Under such circumstances, the player is wise to employ a variation from the battle for the T, using as weapons either the 3-wall or the roll corner. These shots appear to be very similar to the deep alley, but actually die in the opposite extreme of the court from the alley. Like all patterns, the deep-fake deep begins with the struggle for the T:

1. Deep: The player hits one or two deep passing shots, preferably down the wall, to lull the opponent into moving automatically to the back corner.

2. Fake Deep: Employing either the 3-wall shot or the roll corner, the player executes the changeup suddenly but with precision. He then readies himself for his opponent's possible return by assuming a ready position approximately one step in front of the T and one step to that side of the T in which the ball is to be returned.

The player may increase his use of either of these shots if he hits them especially well and/or if his opponent is one who stands back on the T and hits virtually all of his shots hard and deep. In any case, both the 3-wall and the roll corner are highly angled shots and are difficult to execute well unless the opponent's deep shot can be returned from a spot at least two feet from the side wall.

Player hits deep alley shot to draw opponent to forehand back court corner.

With opponent already starting his movement to back corner, player lets ball travel past his front knee and executes 3-wall shot.

Having initially gone the wrong way, opponent is far from ball as it nicks.

THE "DEEP-FAKE SHORT" PATTERN

No matter how deceptive a player's offensive short game, a wily opponent will often anticipate the soft shot and begin moving to the front wall before it is hit. The opponent also may get into the habit of advancing to the frontcourt when he has erred in the battle for the T and sees that the player is preparing to execute the usual short putaway attempt. In either of these instances, a changeup in which the ball is deceptively flipped deep to the back court is in order:

1. Deep: The player begins the point by hitting deep passing shots good enough to force the opponent to make a weak or improper return from the back court.

2. Fake Short: With his opponent out of position in the back court but scrambling forward for the expected short putaway, the player bends low and begins to make a soft shot. At the last moment, he flips his wrist hard and sends the ball deep. The particular direction of this flip shot depends on the player's position relative to the court and to the opponent:

If the player is in midcourt and his opponent is in back of him, he should flip the ball down the alley.

If the player is in midcourt and his opponent is in front of him (within peripheral view), he should flip the ball cross-court.

If the player is in the front court and his opponent is right behind him or seems to be moving forward rapidly, the player should flip the ball cross-court.

In any flip shot, it is imperative that only the wrist be employed to provide the necessary power and that the ball not be hit too hard; otherwise the ball will rebound from the back wall and allow the opponent the time he needs to make a return.

Opponent attempts deep passing shot but mistakenly hits ball too low on front wall.

Player hits deep, either cross-court or along wall, to move opponent out of center court.

Player in midcourt flips ball down alley to fool opponent behind him.

Player in midcourt flips ball cross-court to fool opponent in front of him.

Player in front court flips ball cross-court to fool opponent moving toward front wall.

THE "DEEP-SHORT-FAKE DEEP" PATTERN

An opponent who, in returning a player's short putaway attempt, has been caught out of position in the front court will often automatically run backward as hard as he can in order to protect himself against the player's deep winner. With this in mind, the player can fake the deep shot and leave the ball short and out of reach of the rapidly backpedaling opponent:

1. Deep: Again the player starts the pattern by hitting deep to the back court in order to force a weak return from his opponent.

2. Short: Once this weak response has been committed, the player executes a touch shot in hopes of winning the point outright or at least of taking the opponent far out of position.

Player executes deep passing shot . . .

. . . then hits short when his opponent errs.

3. Fake Deep: Having retrieved the player's short shot, the opponent is now backpedaling rapidly to the T. At this point, the player may use one of three shots, depending on whether the opponent left the ball short or hit deep.

If the opponent left the ball in the front court, the player sets as if to hit deep and then executes a drop shot, aiming three to six inches above the tin to avoid error.

If the opponent sent the ball deep, the player hits the 3-wall or roll corner. Again, pinpoint accuracy is not necessary; the player must be careful to aim high enough to avoid hitting the tin.

It is a common opinion among many racketmen that squash is too fast a game to permit the controlled play that the use of these patterns implies. Such a view is not only wrong, it is dangerously misleading. To be sure, much of squash is won on hard scrambling and pure luck. But at the same time, certain key patterns underlie the game and, moreover, serve as guideposts to the most effective way of choosing one's shots. At the very least, one may say that to ignore such patterns is simply to resign oneself to a lower level of play, regardless of the degree of control over the game a player is supposed to be able to experience in squash.

One often hears that the best squash players are somehow capable of thinking many shots in advance. This very real phenomenon is not due to the fact that these players are able to think many times faster than the ordinary person. Rather, it is that they are more aware than the average player of the essential patterns of attack and therefore can react faster and more clearly. Anyone who has mastered the patterns will admit that the effect is somewhat akin to enjoying an extra two or three seconds with which to ascertain the opponent's court position and to determine his probable movement. The key is for the player to become conscious of what these underlying patterns are so that he can use them more effectively and so gain more control over his own game and the match. This advice by no means applies only to the novice; more importantly, it concerns the advanced player who has mastered the shots of squash and is capable of controlling his game, but who is often only half-aware of his reasons for deciding to execute a standard shot in this situation or a changeup in that. The smartest and most successful players are those who accept the fact that they will occasionally lose control of a point but who also try constantly to reassert their control by returning play to the patterns they choose.

CONTROLLING PACE OF THE POINT

Until now, we have discussed point strategy primarily in terms of its first two components, the type and the placement of the shots the player uses. But one may argue that *the essence of squash strategy lies in the proper control of the pace and tempo of play.* The reason for this is that squash is a game in which mobility and shotmaking are highly interrelated. As such, squash is also a game in which the rhythm of play is crucial. The player whose rhythm is broken is immediately at a disadvantage (1) because he is forced to hit off balance, (2) because he is unable to swing with the proper timing, and (3) because his shots are reduced to a series of defensive reactions. The smart player is always conscious of the speed and spin of the ball, and always makes sure that he controls these elements to his greatest advantage and to the disadvantage of his opponent. Within the span of a single point, these elements are referred to as the pace of the point, and are discussed here. Over the longer term of a match, these elements are called the tempo of play, and will be discussed later in the section on "Match Strategy."

PACE CHANGES

Because of the speed and intensity of the battle for each point, most players cannot adjust quickly to a sudden and major change in the speed or spin of the ball from one shot to another. Against such opponents, the drastic change of pace within a point can be physically and psychologically devastating and should be employed often. However, this type of pace change may not be effective against players of a high level of ability. In this case, the more subtle change of pace should be used.

Drastic Changes

1. Fast to slow. The player begins the point by hitting a few fast, deep passing shots. When his opponent becomes used to this pattern and attuned to the speed of the ball, the player hits a slow, medium-arched shot (almost a lob), which does not travel too deeply into the back court. The opponent is likely to err in his return, but the player should be ready just the same to run hard to the front wall to retrieve the attempted putaway shot by the opponent.

2. Slow to fast. The player starts the point by making two or three deep passing shots at three-quarters speed and with sharp back-

spin. He achieves this sharp backspin by scooping under the ball in such a way that, at the end of the stroke, the bottom half of the racket face has been raised to the level of the top half. He then executes a low, hard alley or cross-court aimed approximately one foot above the tin. The shot gains its effectiveness from its surprise value and not from any pinpoint accuracy. Again the player should be prepared to move rapidly to the front wall should his opponent successfully cut off the deep shot and hit short.

Subtle Changes

1. Regular backspin to sharp backspin. Using the basic ground stroke so that a shot of moderate backspin is produced, the player begins the point with a few deep passing shots which rebound slightly off the back wall. He then executes the same deep shot with the exception that *sharp* backspin is applied by means of the slower, scooping stroke. When executed correctly, the shot travels as deep as those which have preceded it but dies in the back court. The opponent, expecting the ball to come out to him, is thus caught unprepared and often makes an ineffective return or none at all.

2. Regular backspin to topspin. Again the player starts the point by hitting the usual deep passing shots off the basic ground stroke. He then hits a deep shot with topspin, bringing the racket face up and over the top of the ball. The shot should be aimed so that the ball bounces a little before the crossing line of the T. Because of the topspin, the ball rebounds off the floor higher than usual. As a result, the opponent is forced to hit a ball traveling in a largely vertical path with a swing which is almost horizontal. Again the player should expect to move quickly to the front wall to retrieve the putaway attempt should the opponent be able to deal effectively with the change of pace.

MATCH STRATEGY

The preceding strategic remarks are useful in that they tell the player how to gain the decisive advantage over his opponent over the course of a particular point. If the player is to have the best chance of winning the match, however, he must possess also an operating knowledge of how to gain that decisive advantage over the course of the entire match. This knowledge is based on the particular playing characteristics of the opponent, and these, in turn, are comprised of the major areas of the opponent's mobility and shotmaking capabilities in which he is strong as well as weak. With an accurate assessment as to what these strengths and weaknesses are, the player can determine a strategy which will force his opponent to use primarily the weak areas of his game and prevent him from employing the strong areas.

In order to simplify the process of assessing one's opponent, we have constructed the following checklist. The player should apply this checklist to his opponent as soon as the prematch warmup begins and should continue to apply it throughout the match. In this way, he will be able to determine quickly and accurately the proper strategy for defeating his opponent, no matter what ploys his opponent might use or what changes he might make.

STRATEGY CHECKLIST FOR DETERMINING RELATIVE STRENGTHS AND WEAKNESSES

Shotmaking

1. Specific Shots: What particular shots are we both hitting well and which shots are we hitting poorly?

2. Forehand and Backhand: Is my opponent's forehand or backhand better? Is my forehand or backhand better?

3. Power: Does my opponent hit with more or less power than I?

4. Short Game: How often and how well does my opponent use the short game? How well am I hitting my short game?

5. Volley: How often and how well does my opponent volley? How well am I volleying?

Mobility

6. T Position: Where on the T does my opponent stand while waiting for my return shots?

7. Quickness: How quick is my opponent? Am I quicker or slower on this particular day than usual?

8. Stamina: Is my opponent in better condition than I?

From this checklist, a successful match strategy can be formed. The first two questions can be translated easily into effective strategy ploys. First, a player should always hit his pet shots whenever feasible while at the same time trying to prevent his opponent from using the shots he hits best. Second, a player should aim most, but not all, of his shots to his opponent's weak side. In an attempt to force an error, the player may try to hit deep to his opponent's weak side two or more times in a row. However, to ensure maximum deception and the highest effectiveness, the player must be certain to hesitate a little longer than usual in beginning his stroke. This allows the opponent time to at least start his movement back to the T. Thus he is prevented from being able to simply wait in one spot for the obvious shot to his weak side and instead is caught going the wrong way. Even this will be ineffective against the opponent, however, if the player hits too much to one side. To have the best chance of success, the player must use enough variation in hitting from side to side to keep his opponent guessing and moving.

Usually, though not always, the opponent's weak side is his backhand. With this in mind, the player immediately should check whether his opponent is right-handed or left-handed. The player who is in the habit of hitting most of his shots to the left side of the court (the backhand side of the right-handed player) and who fails to notice that his present opponent is left-handed may find that he is hitting to the strength rather than to the weakness of his opponent.

The last six questions represent playing characteristics which combine in predictable ways. For example, an opponent who relies on great power seldom hits the tin, but usually does not have an effective volley or short game. On the other hand, an opponent with great control usually hits the volley and short game well but has trouble hitting hard. Finally, a highly mobile opponent will return many shots, but probably will have few accurate ones of his own.

These predictable combinations form the three basic styles of play, or more exactly, the three basic types of players, seen in the game of squash: the power hitter, the control hitter, and the retriever.[7] From the combinations of strengths and weaknesses comprising these types, a player can determine a more complete strategy with which to win the match. In making this determination, however, the player must realize also that his opponent may not fit exactly into one of the three basic types of player. For these cases, the player must employ the last six questions of the checklist individually in order to make slight adjustments in degree which the idiosyncrasies of a particular opponent demand.

The following are three types of players and the strategies needed to defeat them.

POWER HITTER

The power hitter hits virtually everything hard and deep. He wins either by driving the ball past his opponent or by making him so impatient at the length of the rally that he (the opponent) commits an error.

Usual Strengths
1. Hits ball very hard
2. Seldom hits the tin

Usual Weaknesses
1. Has poor short game, often nonexistent
2. Has poor volley game
3. Stands back on the T

Variable
1. Quickness
2. Stamina is good if given time to make each shot but is very poor if forced to run

Appropriate Strategy to Defeat the Power Hitter

1. The player should not try to return power with power unless he can hit harder than the power hitter and finds success in doing so.
2. Under normal circumstances against a good power hitter,

the player should take a T position a one-half step or so farther back than usual. This provides the player with the little extra time he needs when returning a fast shot to get set and to hit the ball out in front of his body. On the other hand, in those situations when the power hitter is running hard for a shot or is hitting off balance, the player should assume a ready position closer to the T, since this enables him to execute his shot sooner and so steal the time the power hitter needs to hit hard. Under no circumstances should the player lag in the back court after returning a deep shot by the power hitter, as this only leads to a battle of deep games, which the power hitter inevitably wins.

3. The player should attempt to volley if possible, hitting both short and long, but being sure, even on short shots, to aim well above the tin. If the opponent's shots are simply too fast to volley adequately, the player should either aim higher on the front wall or forget the volley altogether.

4. In the ground strokes, the player should rely on the deep cross-court as opposed to the deep alley, because this forces the power hitter to run more in order to make his shots. Moreover, he should use varying speeds on the ball to upset the opponent's timing, aiming higher on the front wall when depth is desired. Touch shots should not be hit with pinpoint accuracy, since this usually results in error. Even when they hit well above the tin, these shots are very effective against the power hitter and should be used often, because they force him to move and cause him greater uncertainty as to which shot will be used.

5. The "Defensive-Offensive" Strategy: The player begins by hitting an apparently easy lob or floating shot, which bounces at about the T. The power hitter seldom hits short and is usually very weak in this aspect of the game. However, often he will attempt a touch shot when he is presented with what appears to be the classic midcourt putaway situation. Thus, as the power hitter begins his shot, the player moves very close to the T and readies himself to move quickly to the front wall to retrieve the ball. The power hitter, unable to handle properly the relatively high bounce of the lob, either commits an outright error or sets up the player, already moving rapidly forward, for an easy winner.

Although this "defensive-offensive" strategy is usually most effective against the power hitter, it can and should be used against any opponent whose short game is either weak or obviously patterned. However, the player should remember to use the strategy only occasionally so that the opponent does not correct the error in his short game or stop hitting touch shots entirely. If, in using the strategy, the player finds that the opponent is more accurate or deceptive in his putaway shot than he originally anticipated or if he finds that he is not quick enough to reach the attempted putaway shot in time, he should immediately drop this strategy and seek other methods to defeat his opponent.

6. Perhaps most important, the player must have good stamina and be very patient. The rallies in a match against a power hitter are usually long, due to the defensive, back-court style of play that such an opponent employs. Consequently, the player must be both willing and able to sustain a high level of ability over a much longer period of time than usual, especially if the opponent is a power hitter who is also highly mobile. Of course, stamina cannot be developed during a match; thus the player must always be in top condition in case his opponent plays the power game.

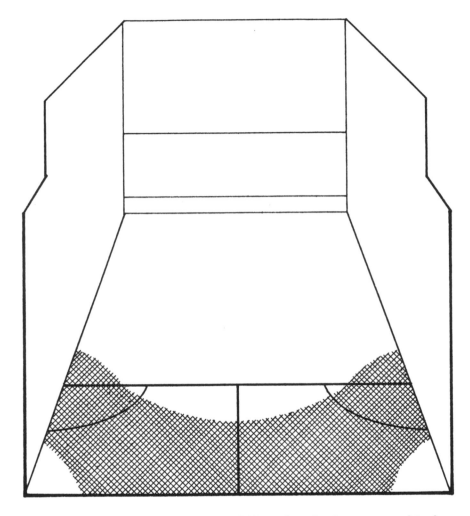

When playing the power hitter, keep ball in deep back corners and in front court; avoid hitting ball into shaded area.

CONTROL HITTER

The control hitter makes very accurate shots but seldom, if ever, hits with great speed. He wins by moving the opponent out of position and then hitting a highly accurate putaway shot for a winner.

Usual Strengths
1. Has good short game—accurate and sometimes diverse
2. Has good volley game
3. Stands on the T, ready to attack
4. Is very quick

Usual Weaknesses
1. Is unable to hit with power
2. Often makes costly errors trying for quick putaway

Variable
1. Stamina

Appropriate Strategy to Defeat the Control Hitter

1. In trying to defeat the control hitter, the player is unwise to attempt pinpoint accuracy unless he is hitting with particular control and confidence in that match.

2. The relative strength of the control hitter is the short game and, at times, the volley. Against such an opponent, the player must return rapidly to center court after making a shot and must assume a ready position directly on the T or even in front of it. In this way, the player avoids the possibility of being caught going the wrong way in his forward movement and is able to reach his opponent's touch and volley shots in plenty of time to return them effectively.

3. The player should use the volley as often as is feasible, as this decreases the amount of time the control hitter has to make his highly accurate shots. The use of the volley is especially important, and indeed is almost a necessity, against the control hitter who himself volleys often and well. In this situation, the player's purpose in hitting the volley is not to win the point outright but rather to keep his deadly opponent out of the center. So instead of seeking pinpoint accuracy, the player should aim higher on the front wall than usual

in order to avoid errors. Volleying in such a safe manner wins the player few points directly but it provides him with a great advantage: it removes the opponent's major, and sometimes only, strength—his ability to volley. Of course, if the player finds that his volley game is too weak to use even in this predominantly defensive way, he should discontinue using the shot.

4. In the ground strokes, the player should rely primarily on the deep alley as opposed to the deep cross-court, since the alley hugs the side wall and thus deprives the control hitter of the room and the time he needs to put the ball away. However, the player must be certain to vary his deep game by hitting the cross-court on occasion so that the control hitter is unable to predict whether the alley or cross-court will be used. Moreover, the player should keep the ball deep, because the control hitter is unable to use his strength, the short game, when he is continually forced to hit from the back court. Finally, in the ground strokes, the player should employ more power than usual if he is at all adept at using the power game, since the fast shot steals the time the control hitter needs to hit with pinpoint accuracy.

Strategy to Oppose the Slow-Moving Control Hitter

The slow-moving control hitter is usually a person who has played for many years but who has lost much quickness and stamina. Such players are not to be underestimated, for they are often quite accurate and are capable of winning a match against a faster opponent. Again, the proper strategy should include (1) frequent use of the volley and half-volley to keep the relatively immobile opponent constantly on the move and (2) the taking of the T position closer to the front wall than usual to increase the pace of the game. Often the power game is very effective, for the reaction time of the opponent is relatively slow. But most important, the player should use what we might call the "strategy of attrition." This strategy is geared to defeat the opponent by wearing him out, and consists of (1) aiming well above the tin at all times to avoid errors, (2) being patient, and (3) seeking to hold the center of the court so that the opponent cannot gain the optimal T position. The strategy is effective because it forces the opponent to play constantly his greatest weakness, specifically, his lack of mobility. If the player is to be successful with this strategy, however, he must be certain to hit shots difficult enough to force the opponent to run hard to reach every shot. The player who is content merely to keep the ball in play invariably will lose to the slow but very accurate opponent.

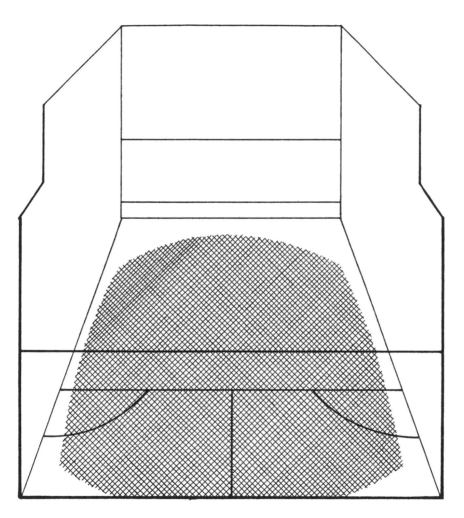

When playing the control hitter, keep ball along side wall and in four corners; avoid hitting ball into shaded area.

RETRIEVER

The "retriever" has great mobility due to his exceptional quickness. He wins by keeping the ball in play until his opponent makes an error or until he (the retriever) is able to use his one or two pet shots to put the ball away.

Usual Strengths

1. Is highly mobile, having both great quickness and stamina
2. Though seldom diverse in his shotmaking, usually has one or two pets shot that he hits very well

Usual Weaknesses

1. Has few very accurate shots
2. Seldom hits with power
3. Though he may volley often, seldom makes the shot well

Appropriate Strategy to Defeat the Retriever

1. The retriever's strength is his mobility, and thus the player should not try to outrun him. Again the player must not be content merely to keep the ball in play; he must concentrate on hitting accurate and effective shots which force the retriever to make errors, or the retriever will run to victory.

2. Because the retriever seldom hits with power, the player should move closer to the front wall than usual when assuming the ready position on the T. The exact spot on the court on which the player takes this position must depend, of course, upon the player's ability to return his opponent's shots effectively. By assuming this relatively advanced T position, the player decreases the time the retriever has to move to the ball. As a result, the retriever's mobility, which is his strength, is decreased.

3. Closely related to this use of the forward T position is a frequent use of the volley. This shot is the primary tool for decreasing an opponent's mobility and it should be used as often as the player's ability and success permit. Again, pinpoint accuracy on the volley is unnecessary and dangerous; the shot is effective because the player attacks the ball, not because he places it an inch above the tin.

4. In the ground strokes, the player should use the deep alley and deep cross-court about equally, the constant variation between these shots being the primary cause of a retriever's errors. Moreover, the player should employ the short game often (especially the corner and reverse corner) since this also increases the variation in the shots and in the court area with which the retriever must contend. Greater concentration on a specific shot or area of the court, such as the deep alley or the short game, can be attempted if the player sees that the retriever is having particular difficulty with that aspect of the game. Again the player should begin by emphasizing the power game, since the retriever often has great difficulty returning a fast shot. However, if the player is unsuccessful in his use of power, he should turn to the control game, hitting to all parts of the court to keep the retriever constantly guessing. In either case, the player must be certain to vary the speed and spin of his shots, as this disrupts the retriever's timing and prevents him from adjusting to any one type of shot the player might use.

5. Above all, the player must be exceptionally patient and constantly alert, because the retriever often will return shots that other players might not even attempt to reach. The surest way to lose to a retriever is to become impatient with the length of each point and to try for a winner before the opponent is out of position. The opposite of this mistake is also very costly; the player who discontinues use of his short game just because the retriever is able to return most of his touch shots requires his opponent to cover only a third of the court. To keep the retriever moving the greatest possible distance, the player should continue to use the short game on occasion, if only to complement his deep game. Of course, he also should be fully prepared to make yet another shot when the retriever reaches a seemingly unreturnable ball.

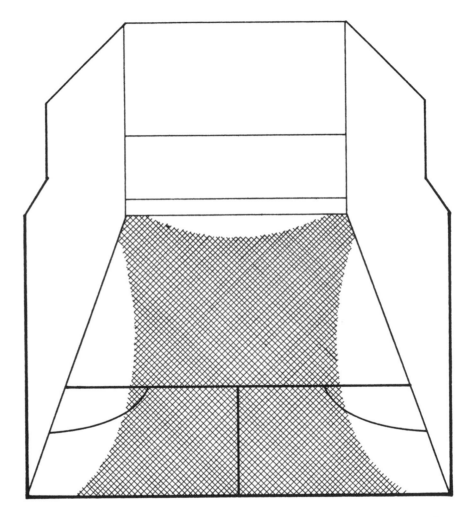

When playing the retriever, keep ball along side wall and use corners and reverse corners; avoid hitting ball into shaded area.

CONTROLLING TEMPO OF PLAY

Throughout the course of a match, a player has time to analyze calmly and carefully the types of shots his opponent is using. As a result, sudden and major changes of speed and spin from one point in the match to another are easily recognized. In making tempo changes over the long term of the match, therefore, the player is wise to begin with a subtle, though immediate, change of *spin,* which is not so easily spotted. In this way, the opponent is always slightly off-balance for every shot he returns though he cannot tell why. However, if this type of tempo change is not working, the player must make an adjustment. In this case, the *spin* and *speed* of the ball and even the *type* of shot employed should be radically altered. These individual rules can be summarized into one general rule concerning long-term, strategic tempo change which always applies:

1. If your opponent is hitting faster shots than you are, causing you to run madly around the court—i.e., if you are being *outthought, slow* the pace of the ball and hit with more backspin.

2. If your opponent is hitting a more controlled game than you are, causing you to be moved all over the court—i.e., if you are being *outshot, speed up* the pace of the ball and follow through deep and low.

TEMPO CHANGES

Fast to Slow

1. Subtle change. If the player finds that he cannot effectively combat his opponent's power game with his own, he must immediately but subtly *decrease* the tempo of play. The player makes this subtle adjustment by altering his stroke. Instead of using the full power stroke, the player employs a scooping stroke in which the ball is hit at *three-quarters speed* and with *sharp backspin.* A power hitter who does not notice this change will hit all his shots off balance, and thus will lose much of his power and overall shotmaking ability.

2. Drastic change. If his opponent is not fooled by this subtle change, the player must immediately make more drastic alterations

to win the match. To accomplish this, the player hits lobs with sharp backspin so that all shots die in the back court. Occasional variation is gained with the 3-wall shot, which serves as a surprise, hard put-away from the back court. If possible, the player should also volley more often, for this deprives the opponent of the time he needs to hit with effective power. Because of his opponent's power, however, the player may find it necessary to position himself a half-step farther back on the T than usual to give himself time to volley the ball in front of his body.

Slow to Fast

1. Subtle change. If the player finds that he is being outshot by the controlled play of his opponent, he must immediately but subtly *increase* the tempo of play. Again this subtle alteration is accomplished by a simple change in stroke. Instead of using a control stroke that produces sharp backspin, the player uses a full power stroke, focusing all body and swing movements to the desired spot on the front wall. In making the stroke, the player should wait a little longer than usual before beginning his foreswing, thereby adding *explosiveness* (power and deception) to each shot. Moreover, he must be certain to keep his elbow in close to the body throughout the swing, as this increases explosiveness and ensures that even the fastest shots are hit with a high degree of control. Executed correctly, this new stroke forces the opponent to make his control shots from deeper in the back court than before and deprives him of the time he needs to hit his shots with a high degree of accuracy.

2. Drastic change. If this change in stroke is ineffective against the control hitter, drastic changes are required. In this situation, the opponent is probably cutting off most of the player's shots as they pass through midcourt and is putting them away with pinpoint accuracy. Thus the player must volley constantly, hitting the ball hard and deep. The player is also wise to volley cross-court about twice as often as down the alley. When seen from behind, a properly executed cross-court volley (arm thrusting forward, wrist snapping at the last moment) looks like a volley down the rail. The result is that the opponent is drawn forward along the wall in his anticipation and then

must circle around the player to retrieve the hard cross-court now landing in the far back corner. The volley is the key shot here, because it forces the control player to hit on the run and drives him out of the center of the court. At this super-fast tempo, the control hitter has little time to execute his shots with accuracy, especially after he begins to tire.

ENDGAME STRATEGY

The endgame refers either to the overtime points of a game or to the fifth and deciding game of a match. It has basically four characteristics, all of which affect every point played: (1) both players are operating at a lower level of mobility than they were at the beginning of the game or match; (2) both players are under a high degree of pressure and are tense; (3) both players are identical in overall ability; and (4) every point is crucial. The combination of these characteristics, in turn, dictates a strategy which has two components. First, the strategy is one in which the player concentrates on executing properly the most essential fundamentals of mobility, shotmaking, tactics, and strategy. Second, the strategy is one in which the player places special emphasis on the psychological factors of squash in determining his choice of shots and style of play. This strategy, which we call endgame strategy, encompasses both the condensed form of squash in general and that much more specific area of squash in which science and strategy are one.

THE FUNDAMENTALS

At the end of a game or a match, both players are having at least some difficulty in moving around the court. As we know from the "Mobility" section, even a slight drop in mobility can result in a major decrease in shotmaking ability and this, in turn, decreases a player's mobility even more. Therefore the winner in the endgame, to an even greater degree than in squash in general, is the one who forces himself to get back to the T after each shot, who sets early for each shot, and who keeps his opponent moving. Moreover, because of the tension in the endgame, the smart player concentrates on hitting a tough shot to his opponent to keep him under pressure but never aims so close to the tin that an error results. These and other crucial aspects of the game are emphasized in the following automatics.

Mobility
1. Move all the way to the T as soon as you have made your shot.
2. Watch carefully your opponent's racket in order to best anticipate his shot.

Shotmaking
1. Take your racket *all* the way back *early*.
2. Shift your weight forward and directly at the ball.

Tactics
1. Play aggressively but never, never attempt a winner unless the opponent is out of position.
2. Hit the shot you can execute best and your opponent is least able to return.
3. Play the percentage shot.

Strategy
1. Make your opponent move to all parts of the court but use only those shots of which you are most certain.
2. Change the tempo of play.

Keeping these automatics firmly in mind throughout the endgame will give the player the best chance of winning the game or match.

PSYCHOLOGICAL FACTORS

Just by virtue of the fact that both players are involved in the endgame means that they are equal in overall ability, at least up to that point. As such, the difference of winning or losing usually comes in the *psychology* of squash. To know, and to be in control of, the important psychological factors of competitive squash is always a decided advantage. The following automatics must always be kept in mind:

Look calm but also determined. Appearing cool but tough to your opponent is the best way to soften his own will to win.

Take a deep breath before each point and relax all muscles. The player who is relaxed always operates best, both mentally and physically. In the pressure of the endgame, this is especially important.

Do not let your opponent rush you into playing the next point. If the opponent sees that you are allowing him to serve before you are ready, he will feel in control of the match, and his resolve to win and to exert extra energy will be strengthened.

Take a short *break when your opponent has won two or more points in a row and has the momentum.* Stalling is illegal, but a short pause is permissible and enables you to break your opponent's concentration and to restore your own.

Call lets. Again, you must play within the rules but you can interpret them strictly; if your opponent so much as touches you while you are retrieving or hitting the ball, you can and should call a let. The endgame is too crucial a situation to take a chance on losing the point because you fail to call a let when your opponent interferes.

Do not get angry if your opponent makes a bad call or if he hits you with the ball or his racket. Allowing yourself to become angry is a sure way to lose in any racket sport. If there is a potentially irritating situation, forget it, and refocus your thoughts on the next point.

Take a second to review some of the essential fundamentals and to return to a state of intense determination before the overtime begins. This is especially important if you have just caught up to your opponent, sending the game into overtime. Without even knowing it, you may let down mentally, thinking that by pushing the game into overtime you are out of immediate danger. But it is precisely here that you are most likely to lose, for you have relaxed the sharp mental edge which originally enabled you to tie the game. If you are conscious of this tendency to let down, you can avoid it, and perhaps be even tougher after reviewing the fundamentals and reasserting your own will to win.

Concentrate on only one point at a time. You will only suffer a loss of concentration if you think in terms of how many points more are left to play, how far behind you are, how great it will be to win, etc. It is always a good policy to play point by point, but especially so in an endgame situation.

If you hit the tin on two points in a row, or in general, if you are not executing your putaway shots as accurately as usual, turn to the deep game, lengthen the rallies, and then try the putaway shots later. By playing only the deep game when you are having trouble with your accuracy, you not only prevent outright loss of the point but you also allow yourself to hit a high number of shots with few points in the endgame being scored for the opponent. In this way, you can practice your stroke and become more relaxed without having your opponent get far ahead. This rule applies any time but is especially important to remember in the first game of the match and in the endgame.

In the fifth game, work hard at gaining an initial lead of a few points and then continue to apply pressure until you have won. Coach Reade has found that the player who gets to 5 first eventually wins the game a full three-quarters of the time.[8] Again, this is a good policy for any game but is especially so in a fifth-game situation.

Scientific squash is a term which, until now, has referred primarily to the approach we have used in explaining the game. But, hopefully, the reader will not let it end there. In every sport, including squash, the success and enjoyment a player gains largely depend on how well the player knows his game and on how well he can apply his theoretical knowledge to practice. Scientific squash is not simply a way of learning the game, it is a way of playing it which enables the individual to reach his highest capabilities. Get to know the game in all its facets, play it with a scientific completeness, and, most of all, enjoy it.

Appendix: THE RULES OF SQUASH
NOTES
BIBLIOGRAPHY
INDEX

THE RULES OF SQUASH

***OFFICIAL PLAYING RULES/UNITED STATES SQUASH
RACQUETS ASSOCIATION, INC.***

Revised to November 1, 1972

SINGLES PLAYING RULES

1. SERVER

At the start of a match the choice to serve or receive shall be decided by the spin of a racquet. The server retains the serve until he loses a point, in which event he loses the serve.

2. SERVICE

(a) The server, until the ball has left the racquet from the service, must stand with at least one foot on the floor within and not touching the line surrounding the service box and serve the ball onto the front wall above the service line and below the 16′ line before it touches any other part of the court, so that on its rebound (return) it first strikes the floor within, but not touching, the lines of the opposite service court, either before or after touching any other wall or walls within the court. A ball so served is a good service, otherwise it is a Fault.

(b) If the first service is a Fault, the server shall serve again from the same side. If the server makes two consecutive Faults, he loses the point. A service called a Fault may not be played, but the receiver may volley any service which has struck the front wall in accordance with this rule.

(c) At the beginning of each game, and each time there is a new server, the ball shall be served by the winner of the previous point from whichever service box the server elects and thereafter alternately until the service is lost or until the end of the game. If the server serves from the wrong box there shall be no penalty and the service shall count as if served from the correct box, provided, however, that if the receiver does not attempt to return the service, he may demand that it be served from the other box, or if, before the receiver attempts to return the service, the

Referee calls a Let (See Rule 9), the service shall be made from the other box.

(d) A ball is in play from the moment at which it is delivered in service until (1) the point is decided; (2) a Fault, as defined in 2(a) is made; or (3) a Let or Let Point occurs (See Rules 9 and 10).

3. RETURN OF SERVICE AND SUBSEQUENT PLAY

(a) A return is deemed to be made at the instant the ball touches the racquet of the player making the return. To make a good return of a service or of a subsequent return the ball must be struck on the volley or before it has touched the floor twice, and reach the front wall on the fly above the tell-tale and below the 16' line, and it may touch any wall or walls within the court before or after reaching the front wall. On any return the ball may be struck only once. It may not be "carried" or "double-hit".

(b) If the receiver fails to make a good return of a good service, the server wins the point. If the receiver makes a good return of service the players shall alternate making returns until one player fails to make a good return. The player failing to make a good return loses the point.

(c) Until the ball has been touched or has hit the floor twice, it may be struck at any number of times.

(d) If at any time after the ball hits outside the playing surfaces of the court which includes the ceiling and/or lights, or hits a line marking the perimeters of the playing surfaces of the court, the player so hitting the ball loses the point, unless a Let or a Let Point occurs (See Rules 9 and 10).

4. SCORE

Each point won by a player shall add one to his score.

5. GAME

The player who first scores fifteen points wins the game excepting that:
  (a) At "thirteen all" the player who has first reached the score of thirteen must elect one of the following before the next serve:
    (1) Set to five points—making the game eighteen points.
    (2) Set to three points—making the game sixteen points.
    (3) No set, in which event the game remains fifteen points.
  (b) At "fourteen all" provided the score has not been "thirteen all" the player who has first reached the score of fourteen must elect one of the following before the next serve:

(1) Set to three points—making the game seventeen points.

(2) No set, in which event the game remains fifteen points.

6. MATCH

The player who first wins three games wins the match, except that a player may be awarded the match at any time upon the retirement, default or disqualification of an opponent.

7. RIGHT TO PLAY BALL

Immediately after striking the ball a player must get out of an opponent's way and must:

(a) Give an opponent a fair view of the ball, provided, however, interference purely with an opponent's vision in following the flight of the ball is not a Let (See Rule 9);

(b) Give an opponent a fair opportunity to get to and/or strike at the ball in and from any position on the court elected by the opponent; and

(c) Allow an opponent to play the ball to any part of the front wall or to either side wall near the front wall.

8. BALL IN PLAY TOUCHING PLAYER

(a) If a ball in play, after hitting the front wall, but before being returned again, shall touch either player, or anything he wears or carries (other than the racquet of the player who makes the return) the player so touched loses the point, except as provided in Rule 9(a) or 9(b).

(b) If a ball in play touches the player who last returned it or anything he wears or carries before it hits the front wall, the player so touched loses the point.

(c) If a ball in play, after being struck by a player on a return, hits the player's opponent or anything the opponent wears or carries before reaching the front wall:

    (1) The player who made the return shall lose the point if the return would not have been good.

    (2) The player who made the return shall win the point if the ball would have gone directly from the racquet of the player making the return to the front wall without first touching any other wall.

    (3) The point shall be a Let (see Rule 9) if the return except for such interference would have hit the front wall fairly and (1) would have touched some other wall before so hitting the front

wall, or (2) has hit some other wall before hitting the player's opponent or anything he wears or carries.

When there is no Referee, if the player who made the return does not concede that the return would not have been good, or, alternatively, if the player's opponent does not concede that the ball has hit him (or anything he wears or carries) and would have gone directly to the front wall without first touching any other wall, the point shall be a Let.

9. LET

A Let is the playing over of a point.

On the replay of the point the server (1) is entitled to two serves even if a Fault was called on the original point, (2) must serve from the correct box even if he served from the wrong box on the original point, and (3) provided he is a new server, may serve from a service box other than the one selected on the original point.

In addition to the Lets described in Rules 2(c) and 8(c)(3), the following are Lets if the player whose turn it is to strike the ball could otherwise have made a good return:

(a) When such player's opponent violates Rule 7.

(b) When owing to the position of such player, his opponent is unable to avoid being touched by the ball.

(c) When such player refrains from striking at the ball because of a reasonable fear of injuring his opponent.

(d) When such player before or during the act of striking or striking at the ball is touched by his opponent, his racquet or anything he wears or carries.

(e) When on the first bounce from the floor the ball hits on or above the six and one half foot line on the back wall; and

(f) When a ball in play breaks. If a player thinks the ball has broken while play is in progress he must nevertheless complete the point and then immediately request a Let, giving the ball to the Referee for inspection. The Referee shall allow a Let only upon such immediate request if the ball in fact proves to be broken [See Rule 13(c)].

A player may request a Let or a Let Point (See Rule 10). A request by a player for a Let shall automatically include a request for a Let Point. Upon such request, the Referee shall allow a Let, Let Point or no Let.

No Let shall be allowed on any stroke a player makes unless he requests such before or during the act of striking or striking at the ball.

The Referee may not call or allow a Let as defined in this Rule 9 unless such Let is requested by a player; provided, however, the Referee may call a Let at any time (1) when there is interference with play caused by any factor beyond the control of the players, or (2) when he fears that a player is about to suffer severe physical injury.

10. LET POINT

A Let Point is the awarding of a point to a player when an opponent unnecessarily violates Rule 7(b) or 7(c).

An unnecessary violation occurs (1) when the player fails to make the necessary effort within the scope of his normal ability to avoid the violation, thereby depriving his opponent of a clear opportunity to attempt a winning shot, or (2) when the player has repeatedly failed to make the necessary effort within the scope of his normal ability to avoid such violations.

The Referee may not award a Let Point as defined in this Rule 10 unless such Let Point or a Let (see Rule 9) is requested by a player. When there is no Referee, if a player does not concede that he has unnecessarily violated Rule 7(b) or 7(c), the point shall be a Let.

11. CONTINUITY OF PLAY

Play shall be continuous from the first service of each game until the game is concluded. Play shall never be suspended solely to allow a player to recover his strength or wind. The provisions of this Rule 11 shall be strictly construed. The Referee shall be the sole judge of intentional delay, and, after giving due warning, he must default the offender.

Between each game play may be suspended by either player for a period not to exceed two minutes. Between the third and fourth games play may be suspended by either player for a period not to exceed five minutes. Except during the five minute period at the end of the third game, no player may leave the court without permission of the Referee.

Except as otherwise specified in this Rule 11, the Referee may suspend play for such reason and for such period of time as he may consider necessary.

* If play is suspended by the Referee because of an injury to one of the players, such player must resume play within one hour from the point and game score existing at the time play was suspended or default the match, provided, however, if a player suffers cramps or pulled muscles, play may be suspended by the Referee once during a match for such player for a period not to exceed five minutes after which time such player must resume play or default the match.

* means change of substance.

In the event the Referee suspends play other than for injury to a player, play shall be resumed when the Referee determines the cause of such suspension of play has been eliminated, provided, however, if such cause of delay cannot be rectified within one hour, the match shall be postponed to such time as the Tournament Committee determines. Any such suspended match shall be resumed from the point and game score existing at the time the match was stopped unless the Referee and both players unanimously agree to play the entire match or any part of it over.

12. ATTIRE AND EQUIPMENT

(a) Player's attire must be white. Any controversy over attire shall be decided by the Referee whose decision shall be final.

(b) The standard singles ball as specified in the Court, Racquet and Ball Specifications of this Association shall be used.

(c) A racquet as specified in the Court, Racquet and Ball Specifications of this Association shall be used.

13. CONDITION OF BALL

(a) No ball, before or during a match, may be artificially treated, that is, heated or chilled.

(b) At any time, when not in the actual play of a point, another ball may be substituted by the mutual consent of the players or by decision of the Referee.

* (c) A ball shall be determined broken when it has a crack which extends through both its inner and outer surfaces. The ball may be squeezed only enough to determine the extent of the crack. A broken ball shall be replaced and the preceding point shall be a Let [See Rule 9(f)].

* (d) A cracked (but not broken) ball may be replaced by the mutual consent of the players or by decision of the Referee, and the preceding point shall stand.

14. COURT

(a) The singles court shall be as specified in the Court, Racquet and Ball Specifications of this Association.

(b) No equipment of any sort shall be permitted to remain in the court during a match other than the ball used in play, the racquets being used by the players, and the clothes worn by them. All other equipment, such as extra balls, extra racquets, sweaters when not being worn, towels, bathrobes, etc., must be left outside the court. A player who requires a towel

* means change of substance.

or cloth to wipe himself or anything he wears or carries should keep same in his pocket or securely fastened to his belt or waist.

15. REFEREE

(a) A Referee shall control the game. This control shall be exercised from the time the players enter the court. The Referee may limit the time of the warm-up period to five minutes, or shall terminate a longer warm-up period so that the match commences at the scheduled time.

(b) The Referee's decision on all questions of play shall be final except as provided in Rule 15(c).

(c) Two judges may be appointed to act on any appeal by a player to a decision of the Referee. When such judges are acting in a match, a player may appeal any decision of the Referee to the judges, except a decision under Rules 11, 12(a), 13, 15(a) and 15(f). If one judge agrees with the Referee, the Referee's decision stands; if both judges disagree with the Referee, the judges' decision is final. The judges shall make no ruling unless an appeal has been made. The decision of the judges shall be announced promptly by the Referee.

(d) A player may not request the removal or replacement of the Referee or a judge during a match.

(c) A player shall not state his reason for his request under Rule 9 for a Let or Let Point or for his appeal from any decision of the Referee provided, however, that the Referee may request the player to state his reasons.

(f) A Referee serving without judges, after giving due warning of the penalty of this Rule 15(f), in his discretion may disqualify a player for speech or conduct unbecoming to the game of squash racquets, provided that a player may be disqualified without warning if, in the opinion of such referee, he has deliberately caused physical injury to his opponent.

* Where two judges are acting in a match, the Referee in his discretion, upon the agreement of both judges, may disqualify a player with or without prior warning for speech or conduct unbecoming to the game of squash racquets.

DOUBLES PLAYING RULES

1. SERVER

At the start of a match the choice to serve or receive shall be decided by the spin of a racquet.

* means change of substance.

Each side or team shall consist of two players. The two partners of a side shall serve in succession, the first retaining his serve until his side has lost a point. On the loss of the next point the side shall be declared "out" and the serve revert to the opponents. On the first serve of every game, however the "in" side shall be declared "out" after it has lost one point only. The order of serving within a side shall not be changed during the progress of a game.

At the end of a game the side which has won the game shall have the choice of serving or receiving to commence the next game.

2. SERVICE

(a) The server, until the ball has left the racquet from the service, must stand with at least one foot on the floor within and not touching the line surrounding the service box and serve the ball onto the front wall above the service line and below the 20′ line before it touches any other part of the court, so that on its rebound (return) it first strikes the floor within, but not touching, the lines of the opposite service court, either before or after touching any other wall or walls within the court. A ball so served is a good service, otherwise it is a Fault.

(b) If the first service is a Fault, the server shall serve again from the same side. If the server makes two consecutive Faults, he loses the point. A service called a Fault may not be played, but the receiver may volley any service which has struck the front wall in accordance with this rule.

(c) At the beginning of each game and each time a side becomes "in" the ball shall be served from whichever service box the first server for the side elects, and thereafter alternately until the side is "out" or until the end of the game. If the server serves from the wrong box there shall be no penalty and the service shall count and the play shall proceed as if the box served from was the correct box, provided, however, that if the receiver does not attempt to return the service, he may demand that it be served from the other box, or if, before the receiver attempts to return the service, the Referee calls a Let (See Rule 9), the service shall be made from the other box.

(d) A ball is in play from the moment at which it is delivered in service until (1) the point is decided; (2) a Fault as defined in 2(a) is made; or (3) a Let Point occurs (See Rules 9 and 10).

3. RETURN OF SERVICE AND SUBSEQUENT PLAY

(a) A return is deemed to be made the instant the ball touches the racquet of the player making the return. To make a good return of a service or of a subsequent return the ball must be struck on the volley or before it has touched the floor twice, and reach the front wall on the fly above the tell-tale and below the 20' line, and it may touch any wall or walls within the court before or after reaching the front wall. On any return the ball may be struck only once. It may not be "carried" or "double-hit".

(b) At the beginning of each game each side shall designate one of its players to receive service in the right hand service court and the other to receive service in the left hand service court and throughout the course of such game the service must be received by the players so designated.

(c) If the designated receiver fails to make a good return of a good service, the serving side wins the point. If the designated receiver makes a good return of service the sides shall alternate making returns until one side fails to make a good return. The side failing to make a good return loses the point.

(d) Until the ball has been touched or has hit the floor twice, it may be struck at any number of times by any player on a side.

(e) If at any time after a service the ball hits outside the playing surfaces of the court which includes the ceiling and/or lights, or hits a line marking the perimeters of the playing surfaces of the court, the side so hitting the ball loses the point, unless a Let or a Let Point occurs (See Rules 9 and 10).

4. SCORE

Each point won by either side shall add one to its score.

5. GAME

The side which first scores fifteen points wins the game excepting that:
  (a) At "thirteen all" the side which has first reached the score of thirteen must elect one of the following before the next serve:
    (1) Set to five points—making the game eighteen points.
    (2) Set to three points—making the game sixteen points.
    (3) No set, in which event the game remains fifteen points.
  (b) At "fourteen all" provided the score has not been "thirteen all" the the side which has first reached the score of fourteen must elect one of the following before the next serve:
    (1) Set to three points—making the game seventeen points.
    (2) No set, in which event the game remains fifteen points.

6. MATCH

The side which first wins three games wins the match, except that a side may be awarded the match at any time upon the retirement, default or disqualification of the opposing side.

7. RIGHT TO PLAY THE BALL

Immediately after he or his partner has struck the ball, each player must get out of his opponents' way and must:

(a) Give his opponents a fair view of the ball, provided, however, interference purely with an opponent's vision in following the flight of the ball is not a Let (See Rule 9);

(b) Give his opponents a fair opportunity to get to and/or strike at the ball in and from any position on the court elected by an opponent; and

(c) Allow either opponent to play the ball to any part of the front wall or to either side wall near the front wall.

8. BALL IN PLAY TOUCHING PLAYER

(a) If a ball in play, after hitting the front wall, but before being returned again, shall touch any player, or anything he wears or carries (other than the racquet of the player who makes the return) the side of the player so touched loses the point, except as provided in Rule 9(a) or 9(b).

(b) If the ball in play touches the player who has last returned it or his partner or anything either of them wears or carries before it hits the front wall, the side of the player so touched loses the point.

(c) If a ball in play, after being struck by a player on a return, hits either of the player's opponents or anything either of them wears or carries before reaching the front wall:

(1) The side of the player who made the return shall lose the point if the return would not have been good.

(2) The point shall be a Let (See Rule 9) if the return would have hit the front wall fairly except for such interference.

When there is no Referee, if the side which made the return does not concede that the return would not have been good, or, alternatively, if the side's opponents do not concede that the ball has hit one of them (or anything they wear or carry), the point shall be a Let.

9. LET

A Let is the playing over of a point.

On the replay of the point the server (1) is entitled to two serves even if a Fault was called on the original point, (2) must serve from the correct box even if he served from the wrong box on the original point, and (3) provided he is a new server, may serve from a service box other than the one selected on the original point.

In addition to the Lets described in Rules 2(c) and 8(c)(2), the following are Lets if a player on the side whose turn it is to strike the ball could otherwise have made a good return:

(a) When an opponent of such player violates rule 7.

(b) When owing to the position of such player, either of his opponents is unable to avoid being touched by the ball.

(c) When such player refrains from striking at the ball because of a reasonable fear of injuring his opponent.

(d) When such player before or during the act of striking or striking at the ball is touched by either of his opponents, their racquets or anything either of them wear or carry.

(e) When on the first bounce from the floor the ball hits on or above the seven-foot line on the back wall; and

(f) When a ball in play breaks. If a player thinks the ball has broken while play is in progress he must nevertheless complete the point and then immediately request a Let, giving the ball to the Referee for inspection. The Referee shall allow a Let only upon such immediate request if the ball proves in fact to be broken [See Rule 13(c)].

A player may request a Let or a Let Point (see rule 10). A request by a player for a Let shall automatically include a request for a Let Point. Upon such request, the Referee shall allow a Let, Let Point, or no Let.

No Let shall be allowed on any stroke a player makes unless he requests such before or during the act of striking or striking at the ball.

The Referee may not call or allow a Let as defined in this Rule 9 unless such Let is requested by a player; provided, however, the Referee may call a Let at any time (1) when there is interference with play caused by any factor beyond the control of the players, or (2) when he fears that a player is about to suffer severe physical injury.

10. LET POINT

A Let Point is the awarding of a point to a side when an opponent unnecessarily violates Rule 7(b) or 7(c).

An unnecessary violation occurs (1) when the player fails to make the necessary effort within the scope of his normal ability to avoid the violation, thereby depriving an opponent of a clear opportunity to attempt a winning shot, or (2) when the player has repeatedly failed to make the necessary effort within the scope of his normal ability to avoid such violations.

The Referee may not award a Let Point as defined in this Rule 10 unless such Let Point or a Let (See Rule 9) is requested by a player.

When there is no Referee, if a player does not concede that he has unnecessarily violated Rule 7(b) or 7(c), the point shall be a Let.

11. CONTINUITY OF PLAY

Play shall be continuous from the first service of each game until the game is concluded. Play shall never be suspended solely to allow a player to recover his strength or wind. The provisions of this Rule 11 shall be strictly construed. The Referee shall be the sole judge of intentional delay, and, after giving due warning, he must default the offender.

Between each game play may be suspended by any player for a period not to exceed two minutes. Between the third and fourth games play may be suspended by any player for a period not to exceed five minutes. Except during the five minute period at the end of the third game, no player may leave the court without permission of the Referee.

Except as otherwise specified in this Rule 11, the Referee may suspend play for such reason and for such period of time as he may consider necessary.

* If play is suspended by the Referee because of an injury to one of the players, such player must resume play within one hour from the point and game score existing at the time play was suspended or his side shall default the match, provided, however, if a player suffers cramps or pulled muscles, play may be suspended by the Referee once during the match for each player for a period not to exceed five minutes after which time such player must resume play or his side shall default the match.

In the event the Referee suspends play other than for injury to a player, play shall be resumed when the Referee determines the cause of such suspension of play has been eliminated, provided, however, if such cause of delay cannot be rectified within one hour, the match shall be postponed to such time as the Tournament Committee determines. Any such suspended match shall be resumed from the point and game score existing at the time the match was stopped unless the Referee and both sides unanimously agree to play the entire match or any part of it over.

12. ATTIRE AND EQUIPMENT

(a) Player's attire must be white. Any controversy over attire shall be decided by the Referee whose decision shall be final.

(b) The standard doubles ball as specified in the Court, Racquet and Ball Specifications of this Association shall be used.

* means change of substance.

(c) A racquet as specified in the Court, Racquet and Ball Specifications of this Association shall be used.

13. CONDITION OF BALL

(a) No ball, before or during a match, may be artificially treated, that is, heated or chilled.

(b) At any time, when not in the actual play of a point, another ball may be substituted by the mutual consent of the sides or by decision of the Referee.

* (c) A ball shall be determined broken when it has a crack which extends through both its inner and outer surfaces. The ball may be squeezed only enough to determine the extent of the crack. A broken ball shall be replaced and the preceding point shall be a Let [See Rule 9(f)].

* (d) A cracked (but not broken) ball may be replaced by the mutual consent of the sides or by decision of the Referee, and the preceding point shall stand.

14. COURT

(a) The doubles court shall be as specified in the Court, Racquet and Ball Specifications of this Association.

(b) No equipment of any sort shall be permitted to remain in the court during a match other than the ball used in play, the racquets being used by the players, and the clothes worn by them. All other equipment, such as extra balls, extra racquets, sweaters when not being worn, towels, bathrobes, etc., must be left outside the court. A player who requires a towel or cloth to wipe himself or anything he wears or carries should keep same in his pocket or securely fastened to his belt or waist.

15. REFEREE

(a) A Referee shall control the game. This control shall be exercised from the time the players enter the court. The Referee may limit the time of the warm-up period to five minutes, or shall terminate a longer warm-up period so that the match commences at the scheduled time.

(b) The Referee's decision on all questions of play shall be final, except as provided in Rule 15(j).

(c) Two judges may be appointed to act on any appeal by a player to a decision of the Referee. When such judges are acting in a match, a player may appeal any decision of the Referee to the judges, except a

---

* means change of substance.

decision under Rules 11, 12(a), 14, 15(a), and 15(f). If one judge agrees with the Referee, the Referee's decision stands; if both judges disagree with the Referee, the judges' decision is final. The judges shall make no ruling unless an appeal has been made. The decision of the judges shall be announced promptly by the Referee.

(d) A player may not request the removal or replacement of the Referee or a judge during a match.

(e) A player shall not state his reason for his request under Rule 9 for a Let or Let Point or for his appeal from any decision of the Referee, provided, however, that the Referee may request the player to state his reasons.

(f) A Referee serving without judges, after giving due warning of the penalty of this Rule 15(f), in his discretion may disqualify a side for speech or conduct by a player unbecoming to the game of squash racquets, provided that a side may be disqualified without warning if, in the opinion of such referee, a player has deliberately caused physical injury to an opponent.

* Where two judges are acting in a match, the Referee in his discretion, upon the agreement of both judges, may disqualify a side with or without prior warning for speech or conduct unbecoming to the game of squash racquets.

* means change of substance.

NOTES

1. Frank G. Menke, *The Encyclopedia of Sports,* revisions edited by Roger Treat, New York: A. S. Barnes Co., 1944, p. 879.
2. Richard Malacrea, Head Trainer, Princeton University.
3. *Ibid.*
4. Jack Barnaby, "The Volley," *United States Lawn Tennis Association Magazine,* 1952.
5. Edwin Reade. Coach, Deerfield Academy.
6. Jack Barnaby. "Percentage Squash," *Massachusetts Squash Racquets Association Yearbook,* 1968.
7. Al Molloy, with Rex Lardner, *Sports Illustrated Book of Squash,* Philadelphia: J. B. Lippincott, 1963, p. 67.
8. Edwin Reade. Coach, Deerfield Academy.

BIBLIOGRAPHY

BOOKS

Khan, Hashim, with Richard E. Randall. *Squash Racquets: The Khan Game,* Wayne State University Press, Detroit, 1967.
Molloy, Al, Jr., with Rex Lardner. *Sports Illustrated Book of Squash,* J. B. Lippincott Company, Philadelphia and New York, 1963.
Wood, Peter. *The Book of Squash* (Van Nostrand Reinhold Sports and Leisure Series), Van Nostrand Reinhold, 1972.

MAGAZINES

Squash Racquets, U.S.A., Salt Lake City, Utah.
United States Squash Racquets Association Yearbook, Bala Cynwyd, Pennsylvania.

INDEX